PEACE

through

CO-OPERATION

PEACE
through
CO-OPERATION

By J. HENRY CARPENTER

30106

HARPER & BROTHERS
New York
London

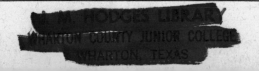

To the Memory of my Mother
Mary Esther Parker Carpenter
at whose knee I learned my
first and lasting impression of the
Fatherhood of God
and the
Brotherhood of Man

CONTENTS

CONTENTS

FOREWORD

~~~~~~~~~~~~~~~~~

IN 1936 I WAS CONVERTED TO THE IDEA OF co-operation and began to glimpse the deeper significance of the Co-operative movement as a force for just and righteous living and as a way toward peace. Since that time it has been my privilege to study the movement in nineteen different countries on five continents. As a result of this firsthand knowledge I am convinced that when we think of a peace which in any sense will be lasting, we must think also of co-operation between the nations and races of the world based upon the Christian principles of justice, brotherhood, equality and love. But these abstract ideas to be effective, must be put into concrete terms. This, to my mind, is done through the Co-operative movement.

In this short book I have set forth some of my ideas and convictions. There is nothing final nor conclusive in the judgments, except as they may be founded upon fundamental religious and moral truths which are basic to all nations, races and religions and which must be universal in their application if we are to solve our world problems. The reader may rightly contest many of my own interpretations but he will find it difficult to refute the idea of the basic co-operation between nations and the rights of all peoples to political, economic and racial freedom which alone will bring us to an enduring peace.

The viewpoints herein developed first came to me as I preached to and talked with a group of 117 men (passengers and crew) on the good ship "Cape Cod" as she was proceeding to the war zone in India and China. A sixty-four day trip on the treacherous ocean in the summer of 1942 gave time for reflection and writing, a kind of relief from the tensions and alarms each day brought.

My thanks go to Captain James A. MacCabe, master of the ship, for the use of his desk and office, and to "Levi" who swept around me, my papers and books, always saying, "Dat's all right, suh, don' move." My gratitude extends also to those men on the ship and the thousands of others I have met in Europe, in Africa, in Asia or in South America, and on our own continent from Newfoundland to Mexico, and from New York to California, who have given me ideas or have tested my faith and belief in co-operation. My apology is that I have not done justice to their insight into life and to their hope for a better world to come.

My especial appreciation must be given to my friends and co-workers who read the original manuscripts and offered valuable suggestions as to changes in the form and composition of the text, Benson Y. Landis and James Myers of the Federal Council of Churches, and E. R. Bowen and Wallace J. Campbell of the Co-operative League. Then my deepest appreciation goes to Mr. Dudley Zuver of the staff of Harper and Brothers for his co-operation in rearranging and rewriting the original manuscript. And finally, to my wife and daughters and my office associates for the many ways in which they helped "behind the scenes" to make the final printing possible.

The book itself is a co-operative enterprise. It tells of co-operation as I have seen it lived and practiced throughout the world. My hope and prayer is that it may in some small way help toward the development of that co-operative world which must be built if we are to have a just and durable peace.

Brooklyn, New York J. HENRY CARPENTER
January 30, 1944

PEACE

through

CO-OPERATION

1

What Is Peace?

THE ONLY DEFINITION OF PEACE IT SEEMS possible to give on the basis of facts is that peace is something everybody wants. Hitler wants peace. The Pope wants peace. The Axis wants peace. The Allies want peace. You want peace. I want peace. The desire for peace appears to be unanimous.

It does not require righteousness or wisdom to wish for peace. We all wish for it. No books nor sermons are necessary to arouse interest or enforce assent. And we are all really sincere about it, for we all subtly envisage peace on the basis of our own terms. Wherein we all fail is in giving insufficient thought to the content of peace, to the condition on which it may be secured, to the laws which must govern a peaceful world. To this matter the present volume is addressed.

We like to understand peace as a state of affairs where we will be let alone, as individuals and as groups, to enjoy our possessions, unmolested by those who may envy us on account of their abundance. We even like to incite such envy in others; that we have more than they is precisely what makes us rich. We like to understand peace as a static condition, with no alarms from without, no anxieties from within. Peace, of course, shall nowise be interpreted to forbid us from augmenting our wealth, and this rule may be extended to others provided their increase does not imply

1

our decrease. In short to such people, a peaceful world is one where little happens, and nothing happens save it be in our favor.

Obviously, such a world is impossible, for such a world is one of conflict and war, and in the destruction attendant upon war, everybody loses and finds his property reduced. Hence popular conceptions of peace are illogical and self-contradictory. Among a multitude of self-centered, self-seeking individuals and nations there can be no peace, and in the end no individual existence. To seek self-gratification and self-expansion is really to will one's self-extinction. To wish for peace along these lines is to crave the peace of the grave.

In the pages that follow it is my purpose to shed light upon the term that is on everybody's lips, the hope that rises from the depths of everybody's heart: peace on earth. In the course of the argument I shall make frequent use of three concepts necessary to the task. They are: love, co-operation and co-operatives. Love, co-operation and co-operatives, I hold to be closely related and allied. Their connection will become apparent as I proceed. A word, however, might well be inserted at the very start in order to distinguish their applications.

Love, co-operation and co-operatives, these must be differentiated precisely in the manner we divide the sphere of living into religion, ethics and economics. Perhaps we make these accustomed divisions too distinct. I believe we do. Life is whole, a single activity. And if we are to live a Christian life, that must entail also a Christian way of buying and selling. There is a Christian pattern of economic activity. There is a Christian pattern for producing goods, for exchanging goods, for consuming goods. It is my contention that co-operatives conform to the Christian scheme, to the world view envisaged in the Gospels. The religion of the Jews does not consist in the doing of special and exceptional things, but the doing of anything and everything in a special and exceptional manner. "The Son of Man came eating and drinking," but eating and drinking in a way proper to, and alas, peculiar to, the Son of God.

Love, I repeat, is a religious concept. It is a metaphysical term. God is love. Love is the sum and substance of all creation, as well as the aim and the intention of creation itself. Love is the law that governs the planets in their courses, the law that determines the path of atoms in the molecule. Love, it is that integrates the cells within the living body. Love is the will of God in obedience to which all nature has sprung into existence. Love is the highest reality, of which human beings and the societies they form are but a part. The religion of Christ tells us to love one another, for this is the commandment of God. We are to love, because God has first loved us.

Now when love becomes enthroned within the human heart as it is in the structure of the universe, I call it the motive to co-operate. In social affairs love takes the form of co-operation. The will to co-operate is the unifying and the integrating force within society. That men are members one of another, that they belong together in a single, living organism, is a condition precedent to all human activity.

The word, co-operate, is highly elastic. It is used in a variety of senses, some of which are nearly polar to the use I have in mind. Hence I must labor further to make my own meaning, which I believe to be the true meaning, clear. In one sense co-operation is unavoidable. No matter who the man, nor what extreme of individualistic theory he may hold, someone else brings him into the world and someone else must bury him when he dies. Birth and death therefore, as physical events, are occasions when isolation-ism vanishes, there must be co-operation here and there. But co-operation, in this sense, surely is nothing to write a book about, and certainly no basis of a lasting peace.

Not even the most aggressive of individualists, however, would so limit its meaning. Even the most rugged of indi-vidualists likes to have someone else polish his shoes, pro-vide his food and fuel for his motorcars, and the more rugged he is, strange to say, the more ready also to turn over to subordinates menial phases of his daily routine. The fact that we do render living richer and more com-fortable for one another by the division of labor is not, how-ever, the essence of co-operation. Conversely it is the spirit to co-operate which renders this division of labor possible at all. When the will to co-operate disappears, and society is rent into its constituent fragments, then the issues of noble and ignoble, employers and employees, masters and servants raise their ugly heads. Society is at war within itself, its functional unity disappears, and each man for himself becomes the sole and only rule.

This, likely, is the state in which our society so dismally finds itself. Of course we talk freely about co-operation. But the word is so often used in a highly artificial sense. If each man's sole and intrinsic interest is to express and to fulfill himself, he may discover it expedient to work with others to secure his own selfish ends. Men are wolves to one another, the English social philosopher taught. So in order to be better wolves it is wise to be a little less wolfish. Granted that man is greedy by nature and by right ought to succeed in satisfying his greed, he can achieve this goal more advantageously by working with others in an effort to compromise the manifold conflicts which in such a world seem destined to arise.

Co-operation of this type, unhappily, is exactly what most people understand by the word. It is exactly this sense that I mean to repudiate. This is rational co-operation, co-operation from the head and not the heart, based on an appeal to reason, personal advantage and selfish success. It takes the form of a planned society, with a multitude of rules for keeping on your own side of the road and allowing the other fellow his fair share of the spoils. It assumes that by nature man is a brute, that the doings of men, in their native habitat, is the life of the jungle, that each man, as God has created him, is an insatiable egoist. Thus the co-operative society is to be an improvement upon the divine handiwork. The co-operative society is a human fabrication, artificially imposed upon human nature, and having as its sustaining motive the individual's self-interest, refined by science and experience. It needs constantly to be supported by force or the threat of force. This, apparently, on a planet-wide scale, is the most that is being hoped for, even by the most sanguine of statesmen, to emerge from the present World War. Such a system of co-operation among nations is conceived as the New Order. It is, of course, the old order all over again save for new bits of ornamentation. The notion that co-operation consists in keeping what one has and in restraining those who seek to grab it, is not co-operation if co-operation be understood as the ethical equivalent of love. Nor is it the basis for peace, if peace is to endure beyond the time it takes to prepare a challenge to the *status quo*.

Co-operation, properly understood, is an ethical motive. It is primarily a spirit, a purpose, an intention, and though it strives to embody itself in human constructions, it will never find its tabernacle in the world's mightiest navy or strongest air force. Co-operation, literally, means "working together." But before men can work together, they must be together, belong together, feel themselves together, comprise a single organism of memory and of hope. Men must be animated by a single spirit, be infused by a common life. All men, whatever their function status within society, must be doing the same work, bent on the same quest, engaged in the same job. Life is a common enterprise; the roles individual men play and serve must needs be manifold and diverse. But none is without honor and no worker is superfluous or trivial. Success for me means success for all, for success by its very nature is an end in which all must share alike. We live together, we prosper together, we suffer together; and not because by our own frail hands and methods we have designed it that way. The co-operative world is not one humanity has devised. It is the world we have been born into. It is the world that God has created. God is love, and co-operation of man with man is but our response to His nature, our conscious acceptance of the nature of things. To co-operate is but to indicate our willingness to fit into the total scheme. And the peace we so ardently strive for is but another name for that total scheme of this created world.

Many of us might prefer a different world from the one we were born into. We might prefer a world whose sole goal and mission was to make us comfortable and our problems easy. There is, of course, no evidence that such is the purpose of this world. So we rebel; we will be gods ourselves; we will set up our self-interest as the purpose of creation. God's world is too mysterious, too ironical for us. We do not want peace His way. We do not want a world wherein the capacity to renounce our rights is just as essential to peaceful relations as the power to enforce them; wherein the ability to sacrifice ourselves is as much an ingredient of peace as the strength to assert ourselves. We do not want a world where one must lose one's life to find it. We do not want dynamic change, give and take, the alternation of joy and sorrow, of tension and equilibrium. We do not want it that way; very well then, we do not want peace. We do not want co-operation.

Some want the old freedoms. If they could be let alone and go back to free enterprise and competition everything would be rectified, say some of our financiers and business leaders. But this so-called freedom has led to the ills of capitalism and these in turn to monopolies, international cartels, imperialisms and all their counterparts of greed, poverty, depression and starvation, resulting from unequal treatment of subject peoples or trade barriers against weaker nations. As a result comes reaction, destruction and all the unholy horrors of modern war.

Others declare that the only answer is in the state. Let its ruler be God; His will the law of society. Whether a kind of Fascism or Communism, the rule of the few or of the many, the answer to our questions is in government or state control. Here again the evils of the Gestapo, imprisonment, centralized management of all business result in utter disregard of individual freedom and initiative. One state forthwith becomes a competitor with other states for superior rights in world commerce or plunder. The final picture can only be superwar because of the superstrength of such states. We are now witnessing the death struggle between such great powers. True, we are happy over the outcome, for the monster we call Germany has been overcome by the giant Russia. But what are we going to do with Russia? That is the question which is plaguing diplomats and peoples. And there is no answer on the basis of either the old free competition or the new statism for both of them end in power politics and eventual competitive struggle.

We do not want peace if we choose this course. What horrors men are willing to embrace in their endeavors to escape reality! Many national or world leaders are talking glibly about a way out of our present dilemma through world federation and co-operation between nations. Yet in the same breath they refuse to agree to the liquidation of empire and zones of influence and cry for an international police force to enforce peace. This is *not* co-operation. We shall not have true co-operation until imperialism, whether political or economic, is eliminated, until all races or nationals are free and have equal rights, until the co-operative economy becomes the basic economy of business small or large, of international commerce and intercourse. Then a true world federation of nations can be built upon truly democratic and co-operative states. When the will to build is present, actual construction proceeds apace.

Because I believe so completely and wholeheartedly in true democracy and the Christian principles of brotherhood and love, this book is written. It fails to do justice to the immensity of the problem or the scope and theme of what has been outlined above. It does, however, present a bit of simple thinking based upon experience and travel which it is hoped may be a small contribution to the wider research which must yet come if we are to create a co-operative, peaceful world. That the essays which follow are based upon religious concepts and quote freely from the Scriptures is due to my conviction that the whole co-operative idea is essentially Christian in its basic principles and must be kept so if it is to be a means toward world peace. We must be specific, not vague and general. To my mind, we can only find *peace through co-operatives*.

Now I have used the third in my triad of terms: co-operatives. The co-operative, I hold, is the economic counterpart of co-operation, just as co-operation is the social equivalent of love. If men have the will to co-operate, they must express it in a certain, specific manner. Their economic life must exhibit an appropriate pattern. A peaceful world is an ordered world, and the order it manifests must be compatible with the sense of belonging together which is the essence of co-operation. Capitalism, as we have known it, is irreconcilable with an organized society motivated by the spirit of love. We cannot co-operate under a competitive and monopolistic capitalism. And we cannot want peace unless we intend to co-operate. Thus by short steps we are face to face with the system of co-operatives. The question, what is peace, ends in another, what are co-operatives?

2

What Are Co-operatives?

CO-OPERATIVES ARE A SYSTEM OF THE production and distribution of economic goods, for the creation and allocation of wealth. Their general purpose, therefore, is often identical with that of capitalism; some of the appurtenances and some of the machinery of co-operatives are indistinguishable from the machinery employed by capitalism. But the rationale, the inner spirit are wholly different. Co-operatives, we hold, are the proper and necessary expression of the will to co-operate, while the spirit on which the capitalistic system rests is that of ruthless individualism and division, tempered though it be with human pity and sympathy, and its inherent rapacity modified by enlightened self-interest.

It may be unfashionable to include topics frankly economic, and therefore strictly commercial, in a book devoted primarily to religion and ethics. That religion should be mute and unconcerned with such mundane considerations as buying and selling is, indeed, one of the faults of our religious thought. It is on precisely this point that the Communists put their finger: it is a sore spot. How can their charge that religion is an opiate of the people be answered, save by treating the sufferings of the people with religious remedies? And these sufferings as the Communists note, have indeed an economic cause. Why preach the brotherhood of man as a moral ideal, then permit, or even encourage, men in their actual relations with one another, to behave as hungry and insatiable brutes. Why extol co-operation as an ethical motive, and then create, as the arena in which any motive can be embodied, an industrial world where co-operation is ruled out as a matter of fundamental principle? With the best will in the world, men cannot co-operate save in a co-operative society. It is vain to endeavor to love one's fellow man in a sphere where competition and extermination are the rules one must accept in order to be admitted to it. Co-operatives are, of course, worldly, crass and all of that; but they are related to the ethical motive and the religious spirit of love precisely as the body is related to the soul. If I am putting the cart before the horse, I am doing so knowingly. It is a more grievous error to nourish the horse of good will, then to find one has no cart of organization whatsoever to hitch him to. And it is my conviction that one cannot be a Christian, if we must function within a society where self-interest and personal profit are the dynamic of industrial life. Everybody must work: the Gospel of Christ and all pagan cults and worshipers of Mammon agree on this point. But there is an infinity of differences in the means of generating motive power to keep men at their tasks. For religion to supply one motive, and the economic world another which stands in direct and irreconcilable contradiction to it, is to breed a conflict whose first result is psychological distress, whose ultimate effect is the ruin of both the individual and organized society. It is only our unholy separation of God and the world, of love and activity, of ethics and economics, that has made this page of apology necessary.

As I said in the Foreword, I was converted in 1936. When a person has a sudden change in the direction of his life, when he has grasped a new truth, he is constrained to tell others about it. Perhaps I have been too much the evangelist or exhorter, however; too much, I fear, of the time of friends has been consumed in listening to me. Those beside me in bus or train, in office or restaurant; even those invited to my home, all hear of the Co-operative movement, "the love principle in action."

My conversion happened in this way. For years I had been a preacher of the so-called social gospel. I was forced into socialistic thinking by my very position, as secretary of the Brooklyn Church and Mission Federation. At Christmas and Thanksgiving we packed our cars with baskets of food and clothing to be distributed to the poor, and up rickety stairs we went, into back alleys; we saw the distress and poverty in which this stratum of suffering humanity lived. One day my daughter, then aged ten, accompanied me into a squalid frame building where a mother and three children awaited the father who was in prison. As we went up the stairs to their one room, she said, "Daddy, I don't like the smell in here!" Neither would anyone else. But that mother and those children had to live there. Others, too, helped to convert me. In those days when we were bottling up oil wells because we had too much oil on hand, an old man, a former preacher, came by to ask for fifteen cents to get one gallon of fuel oil. On this bitterly cold February day he needed it for his oilstove at home "to get a little heat in the room where my wife lies on the bed sick." It was not just a hard luck story. He was penniless, and without fuel.

I could go on and on. Having an interest in people, I could be nothing but socialistic in my viewpoint. Yet I was never a member of the Socialist party. I could not believe that the state could cure the evils I saw. I could not agree that by passing laws we could make a different nation, a new race of men. I was convinced that people had to change, to be reborn. I believed in the gospel that changed men's lives, their thinking, their habits, their purposes and desires. I wanted an answer which was religious and Christian.

One summer the federation secretaries gathered at Lake Geneva, Wisconsin, according to custom. We had a two-hour morning discussion under the leadership of Dr. F. Ernest Johnson, of the staff of the Federal Council. He told us all about the faults of business, of government, of capital and labor. He spoke of cells and nuclei of people who were trying this experiment and that. I irritated him greatly for every morning I came back with the same question: "But what is the answer? What is the answer that the Church can give? Concretely, what can I take back to my community and say to people? We somehow never got to quite that point. We came close to it, but it was always 'yet to be worked out.' We stopped with the cell. The cell seemed never to grow or multiply."

At any rate, I was ready for conversion. I would grasp at anything. Finally it happened: I was convicted of sin by Helen Topping, I was led to grace by Toyohiko Kagawa, I was instructed in the faith by Father Coady[1] and Father Tompkins[2] of Nova Scotia and hands were finally laid on me (they put me to work!) by E. R. Bowen, general secretary of the Co-operative League of America and James Myers, industrial secretary of the Federal Council of Churches. A heterogeneous conversion, surely!

[1] Dr. M. M. Coady is director of the Extension Department, St. Francis Xavier University, Antigonish, N. S.

[2] Dr. J. J. Tompkins is now parish priest at Reserve Mines, N. S. He was formerly vice-president of St. Francis Xavier University.

Miss Helen Topping came to America in 1935 and introduced Kagawa. She came to Brooklyn, brought by our Federation Committee on Economic Justice. For an hour or more she held us spellbound by the story of the life and ideas of Toyohiko Kagawa of Japan. Kagawa was an unwanted child of a noble father and a Japanese dancing girl. His mother was dead. The foster mother was unkind and brutal. His life was one of knocks, sorrow and almost slavery. His only release was to sit by the flowers in the garden, when he had a moment's time from household drudgery and drink in the beauty and fragrance they gave. One day this little lonesome boy was walking down the street. He saw a big tent. There were children in there. They were singing. A sign said WELCOME, so in he went. The missionary read that familiar teaching, "Consider the lilies, how they grow: they toil not, neither do they spin; yet I say unto you, even Solomon in all his glory, was not arrayed like one of these." He then told the children of God's care. Someone did care for little children. Kagawa grasped a new idea. That idea was love.

There is no space here for the whole story of his life since then, of the dedication of his life in the slums of Kobe. Kawaga gave his eyesight, his health, his very life-blood for those people of the slums. He lived with harlots and libertines. Murderers and fiends were his bedfellows. He converted a few, but finally saw that the task was hopeless. It was little use just to sit down there at the bottom of the chasm and try to pick up a few of the thousands who were falling continuously over the precipice. Therefore he decided to go up to the top of the cliff and deal with the forces which were pushing the people continuously nearer the edge until they finally lost balance and fell headlong. Without giving up the individual gospel,

Kagawa became an outstanding advocate of the social gospel.

On his trip to America in 1936 it was my privilege to come in close contact with him. How many times I heard him outline his conception of co-operatives. To him the idea of co-operatives was brotherhood. It was religion being worked out in the lives of people. It was the message of Jesus Christ translated into a practical way of life. It was "the love principle in action."

This was exactly the answer I wanted. Everything I had been seeking, everything I had been grasping for, became plain and clear. I was yet a novice but I belonged. This was a message I could preach. I could be positive and my criticisms constructive. This was the way to increase the values of frugality, justice, honesty, equality, both social and religious, brotherhood, co-operation and love. These are the principles that Christ enumerated. These are the principles to which every follower of his must pledge his loyalty. Every test I have put it to in the years since has but increased my faith in the co-operative plan. Here is a power, a force which will increasingly help to solve the social, the economic, the religious and spiritual problems of our age. And what is more, it will solve them in the way Jesus taught and died for, in the way of brotherhood and love.

Let us look at the actual development of this idea as we briefly tell the story of those early pioneers in Rochdale, England, and their struggles to find and to follow the co-operative system. What those unschooled but highly intelligent weavers worked out one hundred years ago are the exact principles employed today. They have not changed. They have stood every test. Many variations have been proposed and devised; then the "Rochdale"

test is applied and they are judged true or found
wanting. There is a basic reason for this. It is one of
the criteria which makes co-operatives so universal and
so Christian. They were founded on the belief in, and
recognition of, the rights and values of the individual. Thus
they rest on the same base as the teachings of Jesus Christ.
In truth, they were taken from his very words, for those
early pioneers were Godly men, versed in the Scriptures.

The Co-operative movement started back in the 1800's
during the years called "the hungry forties." About 1,500
people lived in the little English village of Rochdale.
Most of them—men, women and children—were employed
in the woolen and cotton mills. Their hours of work were
long, from six in the morning until eight at night, and the
wage was very small—a penny or two an hour or about
forty-five cents a week. They lived in poverty and could
not afford to buy even minimum necessities. In desperation,
a strike was called, and the workers demanded higher
wages. But the owners insisted that they could not afford
any increases. The employees lost and the strike leaders
disbanded. A few of the people who had saved a little
money embarked for America, but the rest could not escape
from their wretched conditions.

In desperation, some of them came together to discuss
their plight. Some suggested a petition to the king. Others
thought a political demonstration would aid them. A few
were more practical. They had heard about the ideas of
two men named Robert Owen and Dr. William King who
had devoted their energies and wealth to help workers like
themselves. These leaders saw that the people who worked
at the machines could not afford to buy the things which
the machines made. Therefore they said, "Let the workers
own the machines." But skeptics answered, how could we

poor, hungry people become owners of the machines? It appeared to be a foolish dream. There were a few brave souls, however—twenty-seven men and one woman in all. They started to save their pennies. They called themselves the Equitable Society of Rochdale Pioneers.

Their total savings at the end of one year was only $140. Certainly this would not buy a factory, but it was enough to open a small grocery store if they would run it themselves. Thus they could save for themselves the profits made by the local merchant and the few cents of their wages would go further. A basement room was rented in an old warehouse on a dingy side street called Toad Lane. They bought a small stock of goods—butter, sugar, meal and candles, and placed them on the crude shelves they had made for themselves after working hours. On the night of December 21, 1844, the first consumer-co-operative store opened its doors!

The skeptical crowd and hoodlums of the village stood outside and made fun of the new store, and even hindered its opening. But despite great difficulties and the open opposition of the wealthy merchants, at the end of the first year the Pioneers had done a total of $3,500 worth of business, their membership had grown to 74, and their capital had increased to $900. It was seven years after they started to save their pennies that the Pioneers bought their first factory—a flour mill. Two years later they purchased a shoe factory outright, and by 1855 they owned a cotton and woolen mill.

The faith of those twenty-eight hungry workers had been justified, though not in just the way they expected. They had dared to dream that workers might own their own factory. But these Pioneers were not all factory workers. Their philosophy of ownership of store or factory was not predicated on the fact that they were employees, but on the fact that they were the consumers who were going to use the goods being sold and produced. This idea of ownership by consumers has proved to be much broader and more inclusive than ownership by workers. It is an entirely democratic principle that the consumer should own and control the producing source of the goods he consumes.

In this way, the little Rochdale co-operative grew. It was not merely luck. Nor was it alone the result of their courage and determination. The success came because these pioneers hit upon certain simple rules and methods of doing business which have come to be the basic principles of the Co-operative movement all over the world. During the past hundred years it has been proven that whenever these rules are followed co-operative societies succeed, and that when they are organized on any other basis they constantly fail.

Democracy was the first rule of the Rochdale Pioneers. They invited everyone to join their society and gave each member one vote regardless of the amount of capital he invested.

To this day co-operatives throughout the world maintain open and voluntary membership. There is no line drawn of color or creed or race. To become a member one must buy at least one share of stock. The person who does not have enough initial savings to buy stock at once can make a token down payment, begin buying from the co-operative, and the profits or dividends from his purchases will be applied toward payment for his initial share of stock. Then, to maintain this democratic control, each member has one vote. The question of how much or how little money a person puts into a co-operative enterprise does not determine his voting power. He is allowed one vote as an individual. This is a totally different principle from that followed by the ordinary business corporation or firm. There the man who has one hundred shares has one hundred votes, while the man who has one share has only one vote. Thus money talks, and wealth controls the policies of the business. Not so in a co-operative. Here the men to be served do the talking and decide in true democratic fashion and control their own enterprise. Co-operatives insist that "men should control money," instead of letting money control men.

Secondly, the Pioneers needed to make their pennies go further, so they started out to buy their consumer goods at cost and run their store for themselves. At the end of the first year they had $160 left. This profit was returned to the members as a dividend not on the shares of the stock each owned, but only to the total amount of goods each purchased.

A co-operative store or factory, therefore, is operated at cost and any surplus left over after all expenses are paid is returned to the members as a patronage dividend according to the amount of their purchases, or the labor they have contributed based on the wages received. Sometimes co-operative societies return part or even all (if so voted) dividends to their members in the form of special services or social benefits instead of paying them back in cash. For example, the Belgian societies have built recreation centers, libraries, nurseries and even hospitals for the use of their members. In Mexico, a certain per cent of the profits goes into the social fund by law. In China, the co-operative federations run their own medical and hospital services. However it is done, the fact remains that the surplus belongs to the members and they have a chance to decide by democratic vote what shall be done with it.

Again, as the co-operative is organized to operate at cost (without speculative profit to anyone), members receive a fixed rate of interest on the money which they invest in stock. The twenty-eight Pioneers made tremendous sacrifices in order to get together their first $140 capital. They agreed there should be a definite but limited return made for that sacrifice in the form of interest. Consequently, they paid themselves interest, but at the lowest rate offered in those days.

This principle too is very different from that followed in ordinary business practice. The return upon capital is not fixed. The reward goes up and down according to the profits or losses of the business. Then men speculate and many times receive very high returns on their investments. Co-operators insist that capital should be rewarded with only a minimum and limited rate of interest.

In addition to these important principles which have stood the test of one hundred years, there are certain other accepted methods of doing business which have been almost universally adopted by co-operatives. Goods are sold at prevailing market prices. The possibility of a price war is thus avoided and the co-operative is protected against the charge of selling more cheaply than other stores. The difference between the selling price and the cost price is what private business calls a profit. An attempt has been made in many countries to tax this surplus just as private profits are taxed. But co-operators insist that this amount is an overcharge which is returned to members in patronage savings, and should therefore not be subject to taxation.

Co-operatives generally have proven it expedient to sell for cash only and do not extend credit. Most co-operators also set aside part of their surplus in a reserve fund to cover depreciation, emergencies or expansion. As education is a vital part of the Co-operative movement, wise co-operators provide funds for group study through which men and women learn the principles behind the movement and their children are taught co-operative ideas. Thus enthusiasm and loyalty are developed and maintained.

A superficial observer might see little in a co-operative society to distinguish it from the capitalistic regime. A superficial critic might wonder why it is that the missionaries of the Co-operative movement get so excited about it. True: an industry functioning co-operatively looks surprisingly similar to the same industry run for the private profit of its owners. Co-operative stores have shelves, with goods piled thereon, salespeople, cash registers, bookkeepers. They give food in exchange for dollars. They aim to sell their wares for more than they pay for them. A co-operative factory figures wages by the hour. It computes earnings at the end of the year, pays interest for money invested and even computes dividends on shares outstanding. To all outward appearances, the co-operative scheme is the same story all over again: the sad story of banking and finance. But inwardly, there is a world of difference.

That difference lies here: in a capitalistic economy, the purpose of an interprise is to create profits for those who own it, and these profits naturally become greater as the share of those who work but do not own become less, or the cost to the consumer becomes higher. Save in the case of a one-man business, where owner and worker are identical, capitalism drives a wedge between employer and employee, producer and consumer: their interests are not mutual but antithetical. They prosper in inverse ratio to one another. Our old-fashioned economists and rugged individualists teach that the profit motive is the dynamic of industry and business. But this profit motive obviously can only be felt by, and activate the chosen few: the few the enterprise belongs to. And in pursuing their purpose they must needs be ruthless, for to share equally and benevolently would imply renouncing the very purpose of their possessions. Thus capitalism cannot escape these evils which many capitalists are no longer inclined to deny, for those evils are but a necessary consequence of the evil principle on which the structure rests. Attempts to bridge the gulf between owner and worker, or producer and consumer, by various compromises and gratuities only widens it and hastens the disintegration of the entire system. Let the workingman or the farmer adopt the profit motive for themselves, and take seriously the rule of self-interest, and industrial or business chaos ensues. That self-interest affords the noblest basis for an expanding economy is true only so long as but a very few know about it.

The co-operative program essays to offset the evils of industrial society or unequal distribution of profit by attacking them at their source. It supplies a new motive for the world of work and merchandising. This new motive is co-operation. Men are engaged in a common undertaking: the highest executive and the most menial laborer, the farmer and the city dweller, are uniting in a mutual quest. The rift between owner and employee, between farmer and laborer, which all labor or farm legislation is designed to seal, never appears at all. Industry is an organism from its inception, and all members of the body share the same fortunes. In the economic household of co-operatives, master and servant participate alike in prosperity and in adversity. It is one for all, and all for one, because an artificial division into the one and the many has never arisen. We succeed, we suffer together, in good times and in bad. While there needs must be functional diversity as there is in any organization, there is yet organic wholeness and integrity. Love is a spirit which animates every member, for love is the spirit which indwells the entire body as a unit. Co-operatives, thus, as Kagawa has said, are simply the love principle in action. And a co-operative society differs from a capitalistic one in the essential respect that it is alive, motivated by a will which possesses and infuses all the parts.

From its humble beginnings in Rochdale a century ago, the co-operative idea has spread to other countries, and its progress, though slow, has been substantial, and co-operatives never retreat or withdraw once they have entered a land and secured establishment within its economy. The Scandinavian countries have furnished, perhaps, the most fertile soil, and people who know nothing about the movement invariably associate it with Norway, Sweden, Finland and Denmark. One, like myself, who has traveled north of Oslo through that fertile farmland with green lawns, neatly painted houses and barns, the hay stacked on wires, as only the Scandinavians stack it, the fat cattle in the fields, can never forget the prosperous and peaceful sight. The town of Ulansaker can tell a typical story. The only store in the village had failed, with debts of 75,000 kroner, ten years before the advent of co-operatives. The creamery had gone out of business, leaving machinery and building intact. Then those hardy Norsemen came together. They agreed to take over the store and run the creamery. The whole village turned co-operative. Everything bought came in co-operatively; everything sold went out co-operatively. In ten years, they had paid back the 75,000 kroner and had paid themselves 125,000 more besides. Every home in the village had electricity. Every front fence was painted and upright. The store, the creamery, the school, the church were spotless and vibrant with life. They scarcely understand what is meant by tenant farmers. These are, in fact, less than three per cent. What a contrast to the situation at that time in our western states where 60 per cent—even 70 per cent—of the farmers in one state did not own the land they cultivated!

Denmark, a near neighbor, has been virtually remade by the co-operative system. It is a small country. Two Denmarks could be put into the state of Indiana; sixteen into the state of Texas. There are about three and a half million inhabitants—about as many as live in Minnesota. And like Minnesota her chief wealth is her farm land. Because Denmark lacks other natural resources, her foreign trade has been the bulwark of her economy. She has sold her farm products abroad and brought back the other goods she needs. The exports of this little country are four times as much per capita as those of the United States and she imports more than six times as much.

At the time of our Civil War, Denmark was in a miserable state. At the close of the humiliating war with Prussia and Austria, one of her richest provinces where two hundred thousand of her people lived, was taken from her. Farm land had degenerated as a result of long misuse. The people who cultivated it were practically serfs controlled by great feudal estates and took no pride in the work they did. Few were really educated. Added to all of this, Denmark's chief export at that time was wheat. The European market was then flooded with cheaper wheat from America. So the whole national structure was on the verge of disaster. The people were discouraged and beaten.

Yet today Denmark is an outstanding example to nations with far greater natural wealth. Their people, by their own efforts, have achieved economic stability and security.

Few of the people of Denmark are immensely rich. But there are very few poor people. She has set up a system of social insurance covering sickness, accident, unemployment and old age, which is more complete in its coverage than any other voluntary system in the world.

Formerly tenants, the Danish farmers now own their own land; over 97 per cent of the farmers are landowners, as compared with only 58 per cent in the United States. Besides, they enjoy an average standard of living much higher than a great many American farmers. She has met the terrific competition for foreign markets and has held her own because of the high quality of her products—her milk, butter, fat, eggs and bacon. The question is: what made this remarkable result possible?

First of all, there was a great teacher who was working among the people even at the time of their greatest distress. He inspired them with a new feeling of pride in their national ideals, their language and literature. He filled their minds with faith in democracy and instructed them how to develop democratic methods both in government and in their business or farming. He preached a new kind of nationalism which emphasized not military glory but intellectual and spiritual achievement. He has become the great national hero of Denmark. Anyone who has been in Copenhagen and has stood before the Bishop Grundtvig Memorial Church, surrounded by co-operative houses, knows something of the thankfulness of the people for a great leader.

Out of the teaching of this great bishop, came the Danish folk high schools where young adults learn how to sing and dance and how much fun it is to read books and discover new ideas. Today there are seventy-five of these schools scattered throughout Denmark. According to careful estimate, at least one-third of the present farming population have taken courses at some time during the past thirty years in these folk schools. In addition, there are 2,500 continuation schools in towns and in the open rural areas with more than 60,000 pupils.

This comprehensive educational movement in Denmark laid the spiritual and intellectual groundwork for both political and economic democracy, which has been expressed politically in a liberal government dominated by farmers and workers, and economically in the Co-operative movement.

Through loans and reform legislation, the government has given back the land to the Danish farmer. The railroads, the telegraph system and the long-distance telephone lines are publicly controlled. Social security legislation has been passed. After the wheat market was lost, the government, through school and agricultural agents, took the lead in reorganizing farm production and deliberately changed Danish agriculture to dairy farming and the raising of chickens, pigs and cattle.

At the same time, the Co-operative movement has supplemented and extended the socializing activities of the government, and has enabled the farmer to hold on to his land and make a decent living from it. This was worked out as follows:

At the time the Danish farmer changed from wheat to dairy farming and raising of livestock, the size of his farm was a handicap to him. Eighty per cent of the farms in Denmark contain less than 150 acres. More than one-fifth of them contain only from one to nine acres, averaging two and a half city blocks, while another 26 per cent of them range from ten to thirty-seven acres. There was little room for pasture or the raising of foodstuffs on such small farms; yet it is essential that each farmer make the best possible use of every foot of ground. Besides this, the income from such little tracts of land is limited; consequently, the farmer must buy his supplies and equipment as cheaply as possible. In buying these vital needs co-operatively, the Danish farmers learned the first real lesson in the value of this movement.

It was in 1882 the first dairy co-operative was formed. Today there are over 1,400 such societies. Their membership is made up of 192,000 out of the total of 206,000 farmers, and they handle 90 per cent of the milk supply and nearly half of all the butter produced. There are also co-operative bacon factories where the hogs are slaughtered and the pork is cured; egg collecting societies, which collect, grade and market the eggs both at home and abroad; cattle exporting societies to help in the business of marketing and exporting; a seed growing association to provide better strains of seeds; livestock improvement associations, credit societies to make loans on farm property, and a variety of purchasing co-operatives to secure for their members at reasonable prices the best quality in foodstuffs, fertilizers, cement, coal and machinery. In the large co-operative warehouses in Copenhagen one could see thousands of cases of eggs, hundreds of barrels of pork products and tier upon tier of butter casks, all waiting to be shipped to English co-operatives or other world markets.

Thus through co-operation, the Danes have supplied scientific methods to the business of farming. Even the poorest have had access to the most modern machinery in the co-operative dairy or factory.

These co-operative activities are in charge of the men and women themselves. The people decided to control the condition under which they lived. The result has been summed up by a former American Minister to Denmark in the statement: "Denmark is above all a land of co-operation and a land whose people are very highly civilized. In fact, no people existing are more literate, more interested in things of the mind, more advanced socially, than the Danes."

There was a peaceful atmosphere in all these Scandinavian countries which largely resulted from the Co-operative movement. They formed a perfect pattern for world peace. These people were happy and contented. They were not grasping or zealous to get anything from other people or other nations. They were gladly making their contribution to the world's goods and produce. They were essentially at peace with themselves and with the world. The rude disruption of this ordered society is one of the greatest calamities of the present war. The co-operatives will be reborn in these countries, but unless we develop a co-operative world, there will be factors of fear and distrust which may make a total rebirth next to impossible.

Illustrations could be multiplied from the other countries of Europe, or on this continent, out of Nova Scotia, the maritime provinces, Quebec, and Saskatchewan; or from Mexico and the South American countries; to say nothing of the great expanse of the movement in our own country which has led to nearly a billion dollar business with two and one-half million consumer-owners.

A very brief review of what has happened in the United States reveals the following statistics: In 1943, one-sixth of all the farm supplies in America, $600,000,000 worth, were purchased through co-operatives. Co-operative insurance, another development, is an important price and service "yardstick" for the insurance industry. One co-op, the Farm Bureau Co-operative Insurance Services, born in 1926, provides auto, fire and life insurance to half a million farm and city members and its premium income for 1942 was over thirteen million dollars. The first gas and oil co-op was organized twenty years ago. Last year two thousand co-ops handled over one hundred million dollars worth of petroleum products. Co-op refineries at Phillipsburg, Kansas; Mount Vernon, Indiana; Scotts Bluff, Nebraska; Regina, Saskatchewan; Mereaux, Louisiana; Laurel, Montana; Cushing, Oklahoma and Coffeyville, Chanute and McPherson, Kansas, were operating in 1943 as the co-ops realized their greatest savings could be made if they stepped all the way into production. Today 296 co-op oil wells in Kansas, Indiana, Texas, Illinois and Kentucky provide crude oil which passes through co-op pipe lines to co-op refineries. Co-op transports carry the refined product to co-op bulk plants and service stations—the entire process owned by co-op members. Seven hundred rural electric co-ops are carrying electric light and power to nearly a million farms. A dozen co-op health associations make it possible for several thousand people to budget their medical care. Forty co-operative burial associations bury their members for half price. On 160 campuses student co-operatives have helped thousands of students cut the costs of education. Ten thousand co-operative credit unions with three and a half million members and $350,000,000 in assets have helped drive out loan sharks and demonstrated that the people can do their own banking.

Here and throughout the world, co-operatives are a vital and ongoing force in the world today with every augury that they will be a more potent force tomorrow. These co-operatives in America have become both a way of business and a way of life. Co-operation is the antithesis of that revolutionary communism which was the bane of ill-adjusted communities a decade ago. In 1930 in Nova Scotia, the red flag was flying over the town hall at Glace Bay. The militia had to be summoned. Sidney, the steel center, a city of 35,000 inhabitants, was a hotbed of strife. Communist leaders were discussing how they could successfully set fire to and burn the whole city. Alexander MacIntire was the president and prime mover of that group. By 1937, however, all was changed. When we visited there, the leader of our tour was this same Alexander MacIntire. He was no longer a Communist, a destroyer, but a co-operator, a builder, a leader of men to better things. The story of his return from Communism to Christianity is a most stimulating and fascinating document. The Bishop of Antigonish said in 1938, "Communism is as dead in Nova Scotia as Caesar's proverbial ghost," and so it was. Former communists were running their own stores, directors of their own credit unions, building their own houses together. The churches were filled, the services real; pastor and people, priest and parishioner knew each other. They had worked and planned together during the week. Their relationship was reality itself. Co-operatives will give the Church, as all forms of social life, new vigor and direction. And what is just as important, it becomes an active and living release for the carrying out of the very Christian principles that the Church has been talking about for so long and doing so little to put into effect. The co-operatives thus become an outlet for Christian idealism. The Church needs the co-operatives if it is going really to build a Christian world. The co-operatives, conversely, need the Church to keep their ideals pure and their purposes Christian. "The love principle in action" may save the Church, save democracy, save the world; nothing else will.

Who can tell us how peace is to be established; how

we are going to develop a world federation of nations except upon the basis of real co-operation between the nations. Toyohiko Kagawa has envisioned such a world in his book *Brotherhood Economics*, and Dr. James P. Warbasse[3] outlined the international co-operative society in *Cooperative Democracy*. This international state will be motivated by the feeling of brotherhood; by a sense of social and religious equality; by a system of production for use and the substitution of sharing for a greed for profit. Can a better definition of peace be formulated? Can the road to peace lead in any other direction?

The united cry of mankind today is for peace. The Church dare not turn a deaf ear unto that cry. The Christian Church must answer, not by itself crying peace and adding another voice, a kind of futile echo, to the world's agonizing din. The Church must answer by declaring positively the way to peace. Peace through co-operation must be our response to the afflictions of mankind.

Next to peace, men want freedom. The irons of slavery rest heavy upon the back of humanity. Whole nations are enslaved, and even within countries supposedly politically free and autonomous, vast numbers of people clamor in unison for economic justice or individual rights, while the subjugated populations in colonial possessions clamor for the freedom which has been so rudely wrested from them. It is hard to determine which ranks first in the aspiration of these multitudes, peace or freedom, for without either, the other is impossible. But in the case of freedom, just as of peace, we so often reach for the boon we crave, without giving thought to its content, or substance to our wish. We all want freedom, deeply, passionately, and it is right that

[3] President emeritus of the Cooperative League of the U. S. A.

we desire to be free. But a spurious and counterfeit freedom turns so easily into slavery, and men are so prone to believe they are free up to the very moment when shackles are locked upon their wrists. Is co-operation a requisite of freedom as it is of peace? This query deserves the earnest attention of all those who are striving for the erection of a free world upon the ruins of so much we must now call past.

3

Freedom and Law

HISTORICALLY, DEMOCRACY IS THE COUN-
terpart, if not the twin, of capitalism. Whatever else
the advantages of democracy, it was designed to release
the expansive powers of science and invention, to liberate
humanity from the absolute power of Church or state.
Thus democracy is inextricably associated with freedom.
This association is historically correct, if freedom be understood in an economic sense, and taken to mean that government keep its hands off business. Capitalism was, and would
still like to be, unconcerned about politics. But this situation could obtain only on condition that politics and
politicians remain unconcerned about capitalism. It was a
delightful marriage, arranged on the strange terms that
the parties thereto live under separate roofs, and while
admitting each other's existence, scarcely speak. It is not
strange that such a fictitious relationship finally came to
an end. The marriage lasted well over a hundred years.
But the New Deal finally brought it to a finish. And the
divorce brought capitalism and government face to face as
antagonists. There is not the slightest chance of their ever
arranging an amicable settlement.

From its inception also democracy had largely a negative significance: its inner meaning was that the ancient
repressions associated with royal dynasties and the divine
Church were to be cast off and free rein allowed for

economic exploitation. But just as government can exist
only with the consent of the governed, so exploitation can
exist only with the consent of the exploited. When this
consent no longer obtains and rebellion occurs, political
power can be readily summoned to curb and restrain economic agencies, and if governments can be destroyed in
the name of freedom, governments can be created or
strengthened in the name of freedom also. There is no
virtue inherent in democracy to make it inevitably the
guarantor of economic freedom. Democracy can be transformed into Fascism by startlingly rapid stages. We have
seen it happen across the seas so quickly that the change
seemed baffling. Capitalism will still be crying for freedom
when the last vestiges of it have disappeared, and it will
never discover that the omnipotent state appears as but a
heroic measure to cure its own diseases. The great objec-
tion to Fascism is that it relieves the disease only by killing
the patient. In order to prevent the abuse of freedom, all
possibilities of freedom are destroyed.

While the Co-operative movement agrees with capitalism
in its preference for old-fashioned democracy, and holds
that that government is best which governs least; it maintains that, for economic life to be free of political control,
it must be self-governing. The co-operatives relish statism
and Communism no more than does capitalism, but the
co-operatives assert that their program is the sole alternative
to the "isms." Capitalism has run its course, which in many
respects has been honorable and admirable. Among its
achievements has been democracy itself, with its conception
of economic freedom. But that this freedom continue to
exist, it must accept restraint and responsibility. And lest
law be imposed upon the economic sphere from the outside,
perhaps violently by the hand of a dictator, it must be

self-imposed. There is but one alternative to external force and that is the spirit of co-operation. Thus law and freedom are opposites only in a mind actuated by greed and self-interest. Love is precisely that motive that results from their fusion.

The reconciliation of law and freedom is a problem that has perplexed men throughout civilized history. Our greatest masters have dealt with it. We may recall a familiar New Testament story.[1] The disciples were walking through a field of wheat on the Sabbath day. They had been so intent upon following Jesus and the crowds were pressing him so eagerly that there had been no time for meals. The disciples were hungry, so they plucked the heads of wheat, rolled them between their hands, blew away the chaff and began to eat.

Critics of Jesus were always with him. Consequently, the Pharisees, as they saw what was being done on the Sabbath day, were agog and wagged their heads in disapproval. Jesus, they reasoned, did not realize what these uncouth and rough men were doing. If he knew he would certainly rebuke them. Finally, they could stand the horror no longer. One of their number, the most important of them all, dressed in the carefully tailored and spotless robes of his office, went up to Jesus and tapped him on the shoulder. Then, drawing himself up with all the dignity he possessed and with an expression of disgust and contempt, he said haughtily, "Do you not see what your disciples are doing? They are plucking and winnowing the grain, which is work, and unlawful on the Sabbath. You should order them to stop, then discipline them for their act." Other scribes and Pharisees clustered around and nodded their consent.

[1] Matt. 12:1-14.

Jesus looked up at them with keen, piercing eyes. Haughtiness left the accusers, their heads stopped wagging. Beginning at exactly the point where they had rested their charge, he went back to the Scriptures and asked them, "Have ye not read?" What a situation that was for these men who were so minutely interpreting the law to be asked, "Have you not read the Scriptures yourself? Do you not remember what David did? The Sabbath was made for man and not man for the sabbath." Then Jesus went deliberately out of his way to heal a man, for he maintained the Sabbath was a day for doing good. What day could be better?

Jesus was thus trying to point out the basic differences between the letter of the law and the spirit of it. There was really freedom within the law. Both freedom and law are absolute in a sense, and yet neither is absolute. There is freedom within law and law to determine freedom.

We are fighting for freedom. An alien race, a foreign nation, is striving to enslave us. There is probably no greater incentive for our nation's entering this war than the fear of the loss of freedom. We are fighting this war for freedom, for economic freedom, for religious freedom, for racial freedom, for national freedom. We must fight to pass on this boon of freedom to our children and our children's children.

Yet we are also fighting for law, for our rights. The commercial man wants to reinstate the laws of trade. The international industrialist wants laws of protection guaranteeing his vested interests in other lands. Those who hold patent rights want the laws of monopoly applied to their inventions and formulae. The imperialist wishes still to control the colonies by laws of his own making. Laws must be defended and enforced even if we have to fight for freedom to uphold them. What, one exclaims, are we fighting for? Law and freedom seem identical yet contradictory. Man, we say, is a free moral agent. Man is endowed by God in a sense with absolute freedom. We are told by philosophers that God limited Himself in giving man his freedom. But how can God, the Absolute, the All powerful, be limited? It is our human mystery on a transcendental scale.

Still, when we really grasp this fundamental idea, it is as simple as it is logical. Man is either free or he is not free. If God gave man only partial freedom in any sense, man would not be really free but would be free only up to a certain point. If man were entirely under the domination of God, he would be merely an automaton. God would be operating a marionette show, pulling the strings, and man would jump around on the stage according to God's whim and caprice. There could have been no purpose in creating man under those circumstances, and the universe would be then nothing but a farce and a shadow. So God made man with the power of free choice. He endowed him with mind, with will, with the ability to reason and think for himself. God is therefore limited in His relationship to man. True, He has ultimate power, He could interfere. He could reach down and grab man, and chastise him and say, "Now go back there and be good." But again, that would deprive man of freedom. God has endowed man with freedom, and unless He wishes to intervene and destroy His entire creation, God must abide by the limitations He has imposed upon Himself. Man must run his own affairs.

That is why I look for no sudden, no abrupt ending of this world of ours. I do not expect the whole host of heaven to flash down to earth and set everything right in a twinkle.

The very act of the creation of men would thus be controverted by God. Man must work out his own salvation in the midst of all the sin, the horrors, the destruction of his misuse of power. God will guide him, will help him, will give him His energy and power to do, but He will not intervene. He will work, but only through man.

Each of us is, in this sense, absolutely free. We can do whatsoever we like. We can satisfy any desire and get as much as we can. Anyone is free to ascend the tallest building and jump over the edge. There is nothing to stop him, except his own inhibitions and knowledge of the consequences he faces. His will is his own, even the will to refrain.

This consideration brings us to the reverse side of freedom, the consequences of the laws which are just as absolute as the freedom granted to obey or to disobey. If you jump out of the window, the law of gravitation will bear you to the street. If you are not saved by a life net or by some miraculous means, your body will be crushed. The law of gravitation is inexorable unless some other law intervenes to divert its effect.

So it is with all freedom. Freedom, though absolute in itself, is relative to other laws, natural, environmental, social or legal, absolute likewise in themselves, which are a restraint on the free action of any individual, of any material body whether dead or alive. There is always a consequence to any act. How inexorable is the law that the "sins of the fathers shall be visited upon the children to the third and fourth generations." Just as inevitable, is the law that the blessings and the strength of character of the parents be passed down to their children's children. Good and evil are alike in being effects of choice.

Up to this point we have been considering chiefly the

freedom and the laws of God, the natural laws of the universe. Man, however, has developed his own code of laws and minutiae of regulations to set up barriers against those who would misuse their freedom, who would flout all the laws of nature and of man. As a result, man has added laws of his own devising to the natural laws of God. Many of these are based on or designed to interpret natural laws. Practically all the religious laws and prohibitions of the Israelites were based upon the actual experience of the people in food poisoning, seasonal weather changes or the like. The list of the Ten Commandments was the codification of prohibitions and relationships of people, one to another, which were for the total good of all as over against the whims or caprice of the individual.

When one descends to the level of legalism, what mass and volume confronts one. The local community or city has its set of ordinances, the state develops its statutes and the nation its many constitutional interpretations, bills to regulate this and that, until there has been built up a very lucrative and voluminous business in advising how legally to circumvent these restrictive measures. In fact, one cannot walk down the street of the average city without consciously or unconsciously breaking some law. Many outworn laws are never removed from the statute books. We have all struggled with the problem of keeping strictly to the law; we have all failed. Almost every time one goes over the upper roadway of Manhattan Bridge, he breaks a law which is posted before his very eyes. When anybody proceeds as slowly as that law requires, the person behind breaks another law by going over the white line to pass the law-abiding driver.

The old prohibition law was an attempt in another respect, to make men righteous by statute. Thousands of well-meaning and high-minded leaders and people worked hard to put that amendment in the Constitution, made speeches, wrote songs, made it a religious duty to back the idea of national prohibition. But a decade later, the strongest factor in the repeal of this law was this very question of freedom—individual freedom and group freedom. It is an undoubted truth that we cannot make people righteous by passing laws. We can demand that they go through certain forms and ceremonies as in the emperor worship of ancient Rome or the Shinto cult of modern Japan, but that does not make people religious. On the other hand, no one would say that we should not have restrictive laws to control the sudden passions, the inordinate greed or the base sadism of certain individuals. Some day there will be passed a new law regulating alcoholic beverages. Just what it will be I do not know, but some kind of prohibition will be put upon the manufacture and sale of liquor. The present orgy of license cannot last. Thus we oscillate, and counteract a present evil by a future evil.

Again, we instinctively protest against all efforts to curb the freedom of thought, of assembly or of religion. To erect such barriers is as old as Assyria and Rome. It is a way that politicians or demagogues have of imposing their will or a means of stopping the exposure of corruption and graft. In fact, how many times has the Church down through history, to its utter shame and dishonor, devised some law and put it on statute books, or in canons, that it might oppose progress or create dissension. The Inquisition with all its horrors made inevitable the widespread inhumanities of the Reformation, together with the hatred and religious persecution which has led to much of the inter-faith chaos of our own day.

One cannot quite conclude from this that all freedom and

all law are intrinsically relative. We can hardly pass it off
with such ease. But certainly no freedom is absolute, nor
is any law that men have enacted. Freedom within law
and law within freedom, though an enigma, is the truth
of the actual situation. That is what Jesus was saying to
those strict legalists two thousand years ago. Religious law
had a strangle hold upon Judaism, and he was trying to
free his people and let them be righteous because of inward
spirit, not outward pressure. This ancient question is
focused in our problems of today; our local and individual
relationships, city and state contentions and the whole
international and world struggle, which has precipitated
the present upheaval.

One day I was in the office of a very prominent businessman in Chicago. He was chafing under the restraints of
the New Deal and its regulation of business. He blurted
out, "What we want is freedom—freedom to run our business as we please." He then went on to say, "If in the
process of legitimate business, a man makes a cold million,
why should he not have it to do with as he pleases? It is
his. Why should government step in and tell him how he
should use it? We must have freedom or business will
go to pieces."

One could believe passionately in freedom, yet not
assent to that declaration. Again it is the problem of freedom within law. Government can become so autocratic that
all freedom vanishes. Witness the gradual creeping up of
dictatorship in Europe. We must avoid that in this country.
Every semblance of Fascism or extreme state socialism must
be checked and prevented. On the other hand, the question remains: is business absolutely a law unto itself? Does
that million dollars belong to that one man who made it?
Did not society create that million dollars, not the fortunate

individual who has seized it? And cannot the community, therefore, take back what it has given? Is an owner more than a trustee? The relativity of all freedom, the social law or the rights of others, become factors here. The question of the wages paid to the people who created that wealth of sweat and brawn; the question of old-age security; the question of monopolistic production and values; the question of national or international rights and commerce have to be taken into consideration. No, that million is not his in that categorical sense, nor should he be allowed to do exactly as he pleases with it. The total right of the whole determines the fragmentary right of the individual.

There probably is no point at which the rights of individuals, in fact the rights of whole sections of society or even an entire nation, have been so rudely and grossly denied as in the case of national or international trusts or cartels. The tribute paid in millions of dollars may be one of those millions that the businessman has made, yet again it is not his. In fact, it means that he has taken lands from the farmer, or homes from the laborer, or food from the poor, in order to have that million. Oftentimes we turn to government; it wields the "big stick" only to find the combine turning up in another form even though "broken up" temporarily.

There is a way, however, in which these cartels can really be broken. This is the co-operative way. It balances freedom and law and is worked out on the simplest basic principles. The story of how the co-operatives broke the power of the cartels in Sweden was told by Albin Johannson, president of Kooperativa Forbundet, as follows:

We have no anti-trust law in Sweden; we only have a law for the government to study monopolies. The power of K. F. is based on the accumulated capital of the local societies and ultimately on the sound finances of the members. The effect of this control is felt not only in those fields where K. F. operates its factories but also in other lines of consumers' goods, for private manufacturers know that if they try to peg prices at unreasonable levels K. F. both can and will start manufacturing this line. An example will illustrate this: When I left Sweden a few weeks ago, I was informed that the linoleum monopoly, which comprises practically all factories in this field, had decided to reduce its prices in Sweden 15 per cent. This was done because K. F. had made it known that if the monopoly did not reduce prices, K. F. was ready to build its own linoleum factory. The Swedish consumers will save nearly one million dollars yearly on their purchases of linoleum alone. With this saving the consumers can now buy other necessities, thereby putting more people to work and speeding up economic activities all around, including those also of the private retailers! We have seen what effect reduction in price has upon increased consumption. When K. F. started production of electric lamp bulbs in order to force the European lamp monopoly to reduce its prices, the result was that the Swedish people made an annual saving on this article of about two million dollars.

The oleomargarine trust, the international rubber monopoly and other cartels were also broken in Sweden and Norway. That meant that the standard of living was raised and that more workers were employed.

In America the consumers, through their co-operative organizations, are also reducing prices and overcoming large vested interest and monopolies. The farmers of the Midwest have developed a large oil industry entirely on the co-operative basis in order to reduce oil and gas costs and to keep the savings in their own pockets instead of going out of the state into the money centers of the nation to increase the savings of the few and by that profit, reduce the buying power of the many.

Late in the thirties the Farm Bureau Co-operatives pooled

their resources to build fertilizer factories. The "trust" started a price war in an attempt to drive the co-ops out of business, but the co-ops rallied their membership and with rapidly increasing volume met the trust's prices and saved their members and other farmers in those states of Ohio, Indiana, and Pennsylvania, several million dollars more than the cost of the factories they had built.

Production in other fields was equally successful. Reflecting the spirit behind these enterprises, the Pennsylvania Farm Bureau co-ops painted on the side of their feed mill at Manheim the slogan, FARMERS HAVE PAID FOR MANY MILLS, BUT THIS ONE THEY REALLY OWN.

These illustrations which could be widely multiplied indicate how the co-operatives, by applying their freedom and their lawful rights, can overcome even the largest cartels and yet, at the same time, make more work and more business. Therefore, they "have the increase" at the same time they overcome economic controls which make millions for the few, but produce misery and poverty for the many. Co-operatives, in this sense, find the proper relationship between freedom and law.

The problem of labor relationships is another aspect of our question. A friend of mine was greatly perturbed by the recent labor regulations. He has been an efficiency expert. His business was to go into a factory or mill and make a scientific diagnosis of the situation. If he felt it was necessary to dismiss a hundred men, he did. Efficiency was the only justification he needed. It was a requirement for the economical running of the industry; it would result in enhanced profits for the owners. Now he is irked that he has to call a conference with the labor representative and review the situation with him. Of course we all know of abuses, of racketeering, of inordinate demands of labor. A number of times I have sat in on impossible arbitration conferences. Nevertheless, the workingman must and will have his freedom, his rights. In return for these, he must and will have to submit to controlling and reasonable curbs upon the freedom of organization and of his demands upon the employer.

We would go through the whole gamut of our social problems. How easily they can be formulated as a simple dualism: farmer-labor, consumer-producer, Negro-white, Jewish-Christian, Protestant-Catholic; these are the problems in our complicated and intricate civilization. Freedom-law: in each case we would find demands for freedom and at the same time discover the balance in the laws of God and man. How wonderful it would be if the farmer and the city consumer could submerge their differences and consent to co-operate! How reassuring it would be if religious factions could agree to differ, and then set about to expend their energies upon promoting the righteousness and salvation of mankind. But that day is a long way distant, and man must yet learn that as between freedom and law, he must choose both.

The position of the co-operator, we believe, is equally balanced between freedom and law. The co-operative system accepts neither the omnipotent state nor anarchic economic activity. Even as true democracy is based upon the idea of individual rights or individual freedom, so in the co-operative idea, the individual has every right and complete directive and voting power. The right of a single individual in the control of industry is based not on his wealth or the stock he may own, as in the capitalistic system, but upon his inherent right and worth as a person. Each owner has one vote regardless of the interest he may own or the stock he may control. Yet he is governed by certain rules or laws. All of these limit his absolutely free and arbitrary will. He must buy for cash. He gets only a fixed rate of interest. He can own or buy up only a limited amount of stock and cannot vote by proxy. His salary, if he is an employee as well as a member of the co-operative, is limited by the lowest salary paid. All of these measures apply to all the members. At the same time, they benefit every individual alike. All of these laws or regulations operate for the benefit of the whole group and therefore of each member of it. To buy for cash, to be limited in interest on capital or savings, to be limited in salary, to be limited in the amount of stock one can buy, actually lead to a larger freedom for each and all, and what is more, to an equalized return of dividends or savings. There is no other form of economic or social porcedure which more definitely combines freedom and law, and yet which does so with purer democracy, or with greater benefits to all concerned.

One vast area remains wherein the question of freedom and law becomes tremendously pressing. That is the question of the freedom we are fighting for. How relative is freedom in the international sphere? The Allies are raising the battle cry of freedom, and yet that is the very cry of Germany and Japan. Germany wants economic freedom. Japan wants the freedom to exploit Asia in her own way and for her own benefit. She demands that the white man cease encroaching upon her preserves. Then while we are fighting for freedom, there is a struggle for freedom going on within our Allied nations. The peoples of South America want freedom from restrictions on land, natural resources and religion laid down in former imperialist aggression. The tribes of South Africa and the masses of India want freedom from the dominance of a minority race which has restricted their education, has imposed rules and regulations upon them, has managed their economy, with little or no reference to the advantages of the majority group itself. Ad infinitum, the illustrations could be multiplied, only to render the question more acute and insistent.

The solution is that there is no absolute freedom. Suppose we take it for granted that the peace will be perfect, that the aspirations of all nations and races and classes will be miraculously adjusted, that they will all henceforth be free to do as they please. Yet, will they? Not even the greatest and most powerful nation is free in this sense, and there will be less, much less, freedom for any one nation after this war. The very magnitude of debt and destruction, the very demand for raw materials will make separate national policies impossible. If any nations, any colonials, get the freedom they demand, they will immediately find themselves drawn into the vortex of international responsibility. There is no absolute freedom, not even for the absolute state. There must be co-operation, not only to procure a measure of freedom, but bare survival.

Within the relationship of nations is the one point where we have not been willing as yet to apply the counter law-of-others to our freedom. The doctrine of national sovereignty implies precisely this denial. The underlying reason for the downfall of the League of Nations, as so many writers have indicated, lies at this very point of the sovereignty of nations. We have not yet learned the lesson that even here we are compelled to renounce absolute freedom for the sake of the whole world, which, incidentally, includes us too. Until nations are willing to come together and arbitrate their differences and agree to make national interests subsidiary to world interests, we shall never have peace. The sole and visible alternative is more war. That again is the fundamental difficulty with war. The hatreds engendered, the accusations of responsibility, the retributions demanded, all are woven into a peace which reflects these very feelings rather than embodying a sense of justice which recognizes the law of freedom and limitation of freedom within the law.

No matter how long the discussion concerning law and freedom might be continued, it would leave us just where we set out: in the cornfield with Jews and the Pharisees that Sabbath afternoon. Laws are made for man, not man for laws. The purpose of all law is to enable man to express his peculiar essence, to fulfill his distinctive vocation in the world. But this is also the meaning of freedom when freedom is correctly understood. Thus within the spirit of man these opposites meet, and their apparent contradictions are blended and reconciled. Man is, by virtue of his very nature, a social creature. He is inherently dependent upon others. Even the most ruthless of egoists relies upon the adulation of his fellows for the inflation of his ego. The most sordid of materialists insists that other men admit his green paper notes are worth a million dollars, for without such communal agreement that they represent wealth, the bits of paper would be worthless. All values are socially created, socially acknowledged, and without this collective stamp they could not circulate, they would cease to be desired. Co-operation, in a low and rudimentary sense of the term, is necessary even that the extreme of individualism should flourish. And without a minimum of law, the freedom of anarchy would dissipate itself in the vacuum of chaos.

Thus co-operation may be redefined as a just and proper balance between law and freedom. And the will to co-operate finds that the magnitude of these factors must vary with times and conditions to preserve an even balance.

Both law and freedom are variable and elastic quantities, but the spirit of good will and love remains constant amid their fluctuations. Law and freedom, with their relative amounts, are like the systole and disatole of the heart. But the heart is identical amid all its functions. A co-operative world is not necessarily a static world: indeed, it can never be static nor stagnant. Like the peaceful world we have also described, the co-operative world is one of perpetual change, but of change within the unity of love.

4

Who Shall Inherit the Earth?

THE MOST INSIDIOUS ATTACK UPON religion usually follows the line of acknowledging that religion is true, beautiful and comforting, legitimate, and all that is claimed for it, then insisting that religion confine itself to its own proper sphere. This sphere usually proves to be small and cramped, and to extend only to the building wherein worshipers assemble on the day of prayer. Even the most rabid dictator is content to have religion free, provided religion does not venture beyond the church door. In short, religion is permissible as long as it is irrelevant. God is to be granted a reprieve from concentration camps and firing lines on the condition that God does not trespass upon the domains secular rulers have staked out for their own.

Unfortunately, this method of disposing of religion had been employed long before Hitler came upon the scene. For generations it was the orthodoxy of classical economic theory. It is usually stated in the slogan that religion is religion, business is business. Many of the churches' most generous supporters have more or less required that the Church keep out of politics and business. The Church should devote itself to purely religious pursuits, and remain unsullied by contact with secular affairs, it was proclaimed: it was to be well supported provided it remain futile and superfluous. What religion is to consist of when it is thus divorced from all the activities men are interested in is a bit difficult to say, though it must be confessed much religious thought was devoted to comprehending this incomprehensible. Christianity was reduced to a system of idealism, a kind of vapid contemplation. Jesus was reborn as a cross between a Greek sage and a Hindu mystic: a visionary who glimpsed somewhere in the clouds the vague outlines of a better world which some day might come to pass. And in the meantime, we were free to devote ourselves to promoting our private fortunes along quite different lines from his.

The results of the scheme are before us. Our Protestant churches and the capitalistic economy stand in the same dire plight. And the double debacle can be traced to the same cause: to the insistence that religion be rendered ineffective. We live in a world of powers, of forces, of agencies, of motives. We live in a world where things move, where men act, where events happen. And unless religion is a power among powers, a force among forces, unless it supplies a motive which moves people, unless religion, too, makes things happen, it is simply irrelevant, and had best be left, in all right as it has been so largely in fact, to the aged, the superannuated, and the infirm.

The purpose of the present chapter is to elaborate further our concepts of love and co-operation. Love and co-operation are not exclusively subjects for Sunday morning meditation, they belong not exclusively to an indefinite and irrelevant hope of the spirit. Co-operation is not a thought pattern in an ideal realm: it is a motive that compels men to do things. No matter how tightly the doors of business are barred against it, it has always managed to slip through the barriers, and has been responsible for much activity even on the part of those who endeavored to exclude it.

Our claim is that good will and the co-operative drive constitute a much more potent force than most of us have ever dared to imagine. Love is a power, in the horrible secular sense that it can build buildings, construct bridges and run locomotives. Co-operation will make a man do anything and everything that man is capable of doing, and will cause him to do it better than will any other appeal. The notion that men work best only where their own personal interests are at stake, only when their exertions serve their own selfish ends, is not only an anthropological insult, but also an economic fallacy. We are paying dearly, and there is more due on account, for our error in requiring that business be allowed to write its own psychology and ethics. Industry has nothing to fear from the teachings of Jesus. Co-operation is the mightiest power in this universe.

Power, these days, is a word to conjure with. We hear of superpower, of the power of a new explosive, of the power of the latest gun, of the power of the Flying Fortress, of the armored tank. Power is a word on everyone's lips. The chemist who can find a more powerful explosive, the inventor who can find a method to get more power out of an engine, the scientist who can tap the stores of power in the atom, these are the men high in the esteem and honor of the nation.

All of this power is being directed to a single end: that is, to overcome the enemy, to fight battles, to gain or keep dominance and supremacy. The power which we have assembled is being used to destroy and to kill. Any thinking man would admit that this is absolutely contrary to the purpose of God and the laws of the universe. Probably one of the most diabolical misconstructions of truth is the application of the theory of "survival of the fittest" to the life of man. That may be the law of the jungle but it should certainly not be the law of willing, thinking, worshiping man. And this jungle, too, is largely a product of man's depraved imagination. Man is beyond and above the beast, and so, by the way, is the beast itself. There is a passage in prophecy which envisions that: "And the wolf shall dwell with the lamb, and the leopard shall lie down with the kid; and the calf and the young lion and the fatling together; and a little child shall lead them." As for man, he shall not kill, he shall not steal, he shall not covet, he shall love his neighbor as himself. He shall even love his enemies. The power of might is one way to gain control in this world. But then there is another way to develop, to grow toward the likeness of peace. That way is to use power together to build the future of mankind in the spirit of mutual brotherhood, co-operation and love. This is the principle which motivates the ideas of power on which we will focus our attention in the following pages.

Not long ago, I was talking with a prominent business-man about the problem of the changes to be made in our world if we are going to achieve the future peace we desire. We finally came around to the idea of the profit motive. He was very positive and emphatic in declaring that if we should eliminate the profit motive from the world, business would be completely disrupted and the whole basis of world trade would be undermined. There would be no incentive whatever for industry or our international economic system. "The profit motive is the basis of energy and generates the power to carry on business, industry and world trade. You can't eliminate the profit motive for there is no other motive of like power to take its place," said he. There would be no "incentive" left. What would generate the "power" to carry on business?

There is no other motive which has power comparable to the profit motive.

For a number of years I have been working and concentrating all my energies in accordance with another principle. That motive is love. Is such an aspiration merely impractical idealism? Were all the prophets and saints down through the ages just visionaries? Is all of this talk about an honorable and durable peace the hallucination of a group of unrealistic religionists, completely detached from the affairs of men? Was Jesus Christ merely uttering high-sounding phrases insignificant and ineffective in the face of the overpowering might of Rome, and even less effective now against the challenge for world supremacy by a group of strongly entrenched dictators? I repeat those words of Jesus: "And if ye lend to them of whom ye hope to receive, what thanks have ye? for sinners also lend to sinners, to receive as much again. Give, and it shall be given unto you; good measure, pressed down, and shaken together, and running over, shall men give into your bosom. For with the same measure that ye mete withal it shall be measured to you again."

There is a sound of finality in that assertion. Jesus purported to be stating a fact. Jesus was sure of his principle, love. He was so positive that if you give to others without hope of reward it will be given to you: "good measure, pressed down, and shaken together, and running over." Is there any possible proof that this is the case? If so, it would seem that the whole world would be running over as a result of the law it formulates. That was said nearly two thousand years ago. It has been repeated times without end or number since then. It must be impractical idealism for it has just never worked, as he predicted.

When I first came to this impasse in my thinking, I

adopted a different approach to the problem, an approach appropriate to Jesus' own scientific attitude. I decided to compare the two ideas on the basis of the results obtained and to see what actually happened to people and humanity as a whole under the working of each principle. My own work with people, with those in need, my many opportunities of travel to see what was happening in other parts of the world, and, I must confess, my insatiable desire to snoop, to get to the bottom of things, to leave the beaten path, to take account of the insignificant items which summed up together tell the whole story—all of these combined to help me on my new course. One of the difficulties was that there was so much evidence on the one side which had been tried, and so little on the other side, that it was quite difficult to render the two judgments of equal validity. Another factor, also most significant, was that it became very clear that on the one side the results were generally negative, while on the other side they were clearly positive. I do not want the experiences and quotations I propose to appear one-sided or to sound like an indictment of one idea and a complete substantiation for the other. All I hope to accomplish is to show a world-wide trend, and to plot out a field for further investigation.

Let us, prior to our criticisms of them, pay tribute to all those high-minded, sincerely and deeply Christian businessmen who down through the years and also today have followed faithfully their highest ideals and principles. They have been kind and generous to their employees. They have been helpful in every emergency. They have been philanthropic in their giving and sometimes sacrificial. They have been leaders who have been willing to listen to new ideas and who have actually put into practice or fostered revolutionary changes in technical proceedings or employee relationships. These men have been and are now leaders who can be depended on to be first to adjust themselves to new demands. We all know many of them. They, too, are acutely conscious of the faults of the system under which they must operate, and willing to join in all efforts to improve it.

We must admit further that the driving force of the profit motive has accomplished most phenomenal developments in the modern world. We have much to be thankful for as we look at the wide sweep of its outreach and the vast coverage of its influence. World commerce and planet-wide communication, the opening of new nations to trade, the network of steam and air travel, the telegraph, the cable lines, the radio and so much more have been due primarily to this single force. The average high standard of living, in certain countries at least, and its counterparts in the advance of education, of great endowments for medicine, for sciences, physical and social, the building of institutions for every kind of relief, all of this remarkable philanthropy has been largely the result of the application of the profit motive to business, industry and trade. Not without a measure of plausibility do the profit advocates say, let us alone. If we could only be assured of freedom, we would build a world beyond the dreams of romancers, a world of luxurious living and enforced peace. Why do people we have done so much for continually rise up to thwart us in our achievements and to condemn the very privileges and advantages we have bestowed?

There is the very nub of our question. It is the point in our course where we commence to get a "sight of the sun" and when the sunlight fully shines we shall have the clarity of vision we have been groping for through all the clouds of uncertainty and indecision. Why do citizens rise up and demand release from their nation's vaunted benefits? Why does the workman, the farmer, form unions and associations to fight the very hand which is pouring these bounties upon them? Why do whole nations allow themselves to be dominated by a demagogue and be aroused to murder, rapine and sadism? Why do wars and destruction continually come to mar and deface vast sections of the earth? And furthermore, why does the intensity of this struggle grow progressively more devastating, the loss of life more and more appalling, the cry of suffering more widespread, rising up from the farthest corners of the earth, from the jungles of Africa and Burma to the bleakness of Spitsbergen, or from the smallest island in the sea to the vast steppes of Russia?

There must be some reason for such dissatisfaction and revolt, and some other way, some other motive to rule the affairs of men. The results of any fair inquiry are not entirely favorable. There is a rumbling as of the approaching eruption of a volcano. "The eruption is upon us. Save us, ere we all perish." That is the cry of businessmen as well as of total populations. We do not choose to perish but neither do we want to change our ways. Nothing can take the place of the profit motive, come what may.

Let us, therefore, examine the other side of the issue, to seek there a fresh answer to our questions. How actually has the profit motive advantaged the people it has served? Take the reputed high standard of living in America for example. President Roosevelt in his inaugural address of January, 1937, declared, "I see millions of families trying to live on incomes so meager that the pall of family disaster hangs over them day by day. . . . I see one-third of a nation ill-housed, ill-clad, ill-nourished." How came the advocates of the profit motive to overlook this segment, by no means microscopic? A large section of humanity, even in America, is rising up and demanding, "Why has this 'standard of living' not included us?" Add to this submerged third those millions more who are balanced precariously on the border-line, who have just enough to eat and to wear but do not have any extra, and we find an aspect of the profit economy which is not so pleasant to behold.

If we go into the slums, to those poverty-stricken areas of any great city in America, we see for ourselves the emaciated children, the sickly mothers and the criminal youth. We smell the sickening odors of hallways and alleys, see the sunless rooms, the common toilets, the shivering, crying child in the raw cold of a heatless flat. These situations cannot be viewed as simply opportunities for charity, occasions for pulling out a checkbook and making a generous gift while the smell still lingers in the nostrils and tears still fill the eyes. Such relief is but superficial. The evil is a result of our present economic system. This is something which must be changed; it presents a problem that must be solved. Our nation cannot go on with this as a part of it. No light is to be gained by closing one's eyes.

It is not only in the poverty of the slums, however, that we discover a problem. Let us go to the farms of the Middle West where land mortgages have been foreclosed under the tillers of the soil, where erstwhile respectable farmers have become "tenants" and the "poor whites" of the Dust Bowl. Let us visit the sharecroppers of the South who plant, hoe and pick cotton but, "who don't have a cotton sheet to put on the bed, or a cotton cloth to put around their loins." That is a quotation from a southern doctor who added, describing his professional difficulties, "What is the use of my diagnosing tuberculosis when there are no fresh vegetables, no milk, no meat, not even a decent place to rest, no, not the time to rest, for then there would be stark starvation?" Can these things be in our own free land? Yes, all of this and much more, much worse.

The situation was well summed up by an inter-faith statement signed by one hundred of the highest officials in the Catholic, Jewish, and Protestant religions. This statement was the result of a three-day conference in Washington, during which time government and church leaders of all faiths presented papers and discussed the depression and its consequent human suffering. The final signed declaration stated in clear terse sentences that: "In terms of economic life, our tragedy is due to failure to distribute the income of production widely enough to enable us to end poverty. Too much money has gone to the few. Too little has gone to the many. Too much has gone to interest and dividends. Too little has gone to the many in return for work. Some industries have gained unfairly at the expense of other industries."[1] Thus our economic system has resulted in depression, poverty and finally war. To have failed to see its malevolent effects one must needs be blind or have lived in complete isolation from his kind. One day during the recent depression, three young girls came into my office, out of work and money. I asked them what they were living on and they told me, "bananas." They could buy six for five cents. For four days they had three bananas and a quart of milk each day among them. Yet in that morning's paper I had read that whole shiploads of bananas were being dumped into the ocean off Baltimore harbor to keep up the price.

During those experimental years, we were plowing under

[1] Information Service, Federal Council. Vol. XVIII, No. 22, July 3, 1939.

grain, the farmers were burning corn in their furnaces because no one would buy it. Fruit was left to rot on the trees for there was no profit in marketing it. A world economic conference held in Italy and called to discuss the question of the problem of wheat surpluses decided nothing could be done until we got rid of the millions of bushels of wheat we had on hand. At that very moment millions of people were starving throughout the world for lack of those bushels of wheat. It is not wholly fantastic, I believe, to say that if we had consented to give away that wheat to the starving, that act might have averted the war which is now devastating us. Impossible, such foolishness, I hear some one retort. It would have disrupted the whole world economy. Just let us ponder one question: where is that world economy today? World economy is made for man; to make man serve its end is to destroy both.

The greed for profit has not only controlled national policies, it has led to imperialism on a world-wide scale. This imperialism is not only political; it is economic as well. We in America are prone to look at England and say, We have no imperialism in America. One certainly is glad to admit that our colonial policy has been very broad and generous in the case of both Cuba and the Philippines. The recent free trade policy promoted so vigorously by Secretary Hull and the present administration has been most significant. This is a step in the right direction. Nevertheless, the tentacles of economic imperialism are many and long. The recent revelations of Thurman Arnold of the Attorney General's office on international agreements by American businessmen with enemy industry, or the report of Governor Tugwell on our indefensible colonial policy in Puerto Rico are proofs of this statement. All imperialisms are centered in the one motive for return, for profit.

Millions are taken from other nations and these millions are stuffed into the coffers of nations in power and control.

Let me say it not in my own phrases, but in the honest, clear and straightforward words of Madame Chiang Kaishek in her book *China Shall Rise Again*.[2]

It must be remembered that while impartial, justice-loving Americans did try to . . . aid China in relief work, others in America amassed profits by selling Japan the necessities of war which enabled her to continue her destruction of Chinese life and property. Eighty per cent of Japan's war supplies came from America . . . and 95 per cent of the aviation gasoline which was used by Japan in her ruthless and indiscriminate bombing was American.

And it can be added now that these same products and gasoline upon which "others in America amassed profits" were used to kill American youth, to destroy American property from Pearl Harbor to Bataan and then in the Coral Sea and the Solomon Islands. Of course, Japan wrested from the United States and Great Britain other sources of supplies but in the beginning she used the very materials we sent her and upon which we made our profits. Can any businessman look at these facts and still say the profit motive should ever again be allowed a free hand, or that the profit motive must continue as the dynamic and the motive behind international trade?

The problem of colonies and the rights of native majorities, whether it be in French Equatorial Africa, the Gold Coast, the Union of South Africa, the Belgian Congo, India, Puerto Rico or French Indo-China, is the same everywhere. It is the result of a policy of keeping the natives repressed and enslaved, of keeping them in hand so as to have cheap labor with which to exploit the land,

[2] See p. 349.

the mines, the forests and all the natural resources of these countries possessed by force. As Dr. Edgar H. Brooks, in his book, *The Color Problem of South Africa*, points out this policy must be enforced by a "legalized despotism,"[3] controlled by the minority race, the European white, and in which the native, whether he be black, brown or yellow, has no choice nor voice. Dr. Brooks then goes on to say, "All over the world, non-European populations are clamoring for greater rights. The choice which faces . . . the surplus population of China, Japan and India . . . is essentially the choice which faces South Africa; and in each case an attempt is being made to evade, or at least postpone, the issue."[4]

The same author states in another place that the policy seems to be that the native "must continue to be kept in a state of subjection." His liberties must be curtailed; his education must be limited. For instance, in South Africa, over ten million pounds was spent on European (white) education, while less than one million pounds was spent on native education though the native population was three times as large.[5] In India, "90% of the people are still illiterate, her industrial resources are largely undeveloped and the great majority of her people live in the most abject poverty, with the usual concomitants of disease and low physical vitality. . . . The majority of the people get only two cents a day."[6]

Quotations and illustration could be multiplied. No more are required, however, to pronounce judgment as to the

[3] *Op. cit.*, p. 104.
[4] *Op. cit.*, p. 177.
[5] Official Year Book, Union of South Africa, p. 289.
[6] "India and the War," by Kate L. Mitchell, *Amerasia*, 125 E. 22nd St., New York, N. Y.

poverty, the disease, the illiteracy, the discrimination, the duplicity and finally the open conflict itself which have followed the unrestrained employment of the profit motive. The greed for gain is indubitably responsible for an amazingly large proportion of the calamity and suffering in the world, from which in turn and in reprisal, issue the hatreds, the revolutions, the wars that decimate the world. Dr. Brooks makes a most striking statement. He speaks of "the pathetic way in which men cling to what in their heart of hearts they know is not true because they cannot bring themselves to admit that it is untrue."[7] This so clearly sums up the case regarding the claims of the profit motive. We cannot resolve to renounce it, though its condemnation is on many lips and in vastly more hearts.

Is there any motive to take its place? Will the wheels of industry stop when dollars cease being the fuel for its engines? What motive can supplant the love of money? Our answer is the power inherent in the idea of working together with and for others. Quotations from well-known leaders may help to clarify the power which resides in love and brotherhood applied to business and to convince the skeptical of the absolute necessity for substituting this power for the profit motive.

Listen first to Vice-President Wallace. In his book, *Whose Constitution*, he declares:

Capitalism, while financially stronger today than ever before, is becoming more and more spiritually bankrupt. . . . In the economic world it is inevitable that more and more emphasis is going to be laid on the idea of co-operation as distinguished from free competition.[8]

[7] See p. 53.
[8] Reynal & Hitchcock, New York, pp. 309, 313.

Here, also, Congressman Jerry Voorhis, in *The Morale of Democracy*:

> Co-operatives are inherently built on spiritual motives—they are the most Christian of business institutions. They cannot be selfish and succeed. Some men insist that we must have competition. Undoubtedly, that is true. But there can be competition for something other than profit, or than control of other men. There can be competition to accomplish something higher and better than getting money. Either this is true or else everything that has been taught us by the forces of Christianity is a lie. But it is not a lie.[9]

A hundred more such statements which could be produced from China, South Africa, Norway, Sweden, Denmark, Finland, England, Ireland, Mexico and even from Germany, Italy and Japan in their days of freedom. In fact, I have had the privilege of seeing the co-operative system in operation in most of these countries. I have seen the people of Nova Scotia, in dire poverty while under the control of the profit motive, break loose from this slavery and through the method of co-operation, rise out of their poverty and eliminate bad housing, disease and illiteracy by the simple application of a new reason for doing things. Almost overnight prosperity became more general than it had during a hundred years of monopoly and profiteering. The hardest obstacles co-operatives had to overcome were the forces of economic reaction. The errors of the past are indeed always the most potent enemies of present and future progress. From Africa the story comes of Mxeka and Moquerana where natives discovered the same idea and found that it worked.[10] The farmers of our own Middle

[9] The Greystone Press, New York, pp. 84-85.
[10] The story is told in *Race and Economics in South Africa*, by W. J. Ballinger published by the Hogarth Press, London, p. 57.

West applied the co-operative principle to their needs for fertilizer, oil and gasoline, feed and grain, and many other items. Joshua K. Bolles raises the issue of world trade on this same basis and maintains "that non-profit trade on an international scale would do more to maintain friendly relations among the peoples of the world than all the diplomats of all the great nations."[11]

There is more power in the motive of mutual aid and of collaborating with others than those who have never tried it are willing to believe. Strange though it seems to us who have been nourished on false theories and erroneous views of human nature, a man will work harder for others than he will for himself, and a co-operative enterprise is not only a solvent for egoism, but a key to unlocked, unknown and incredibly vast stores of physical energy. We are not suggesting aimless and undirected altruism: co-operatives are as far removed from sentimentalism as the most ruthless capitalism. What we are suggesting is mutual helpfulness. Co-operatives use capital and pay a set rate of interest, but the additional profit is returned to those who earned it, either in making, buying or selling. The question of goods or trade then becomes not how little we can give, but how much we can give for the money. Thus industry is based on production for use and not production for profit; there is more industry and more goods to use.

The remarkable happening is foretold by the Bible verse quoted before, "Give and it shall be given unto you, good measure, pressed down, and shaken together, and running over." The prospect of human need everywhere being satisfied is nothing to be afraid of. The elimination

[11] *The People's Business,* by Joshua K. Bolles, Harper & Brothers, New York.

of poverty will make more business. Universal education and freedom for the people of India would make such demands upon British industry as England has never known. The good old days businessmen sigh for, lie ahead if they only knew it. The people who are held in subjection and poverty constitute the problem. They cost money, they drain away wealth, for relief and crime and disease, they are the greatest tax on business. Find the way to relieve their distress, to raise their standard of living, and you have created a new buying power which present production capacity could scarcely satisfy. From a practical standpoint the electrical equipment companies could well afford to install electricity in every farmhouse in the United States just for the sake of the volume of business that would ensue for them. At the same time, they could reduce their costs to all consumers because of the total volume. These industrial concerns, of course, do not see it that way, so the farmer is forced to put in his own co-operative lines and will soon own the plants producing his farm machinery. Selfishness and greed always end at the opposite point from what they expected. The more we give and do for others, on the contrary, in honest sharing and service, the more the demands upon us and the larger the return, and what is more important, the greater the satisfaction and the stronger the incentive to go on. Once launched upon this course, there is no turning back, no stopping.

This principle was clearly illustrated in the beginnings of co-operative world trade before the war. It may be that these plain people, the two hundred million members of co-operatives in the thirty-nine countries of the world have pointed the way. They have done it without any bloodshed, without tariffs or trade boundaries. They have built a "league of peoples" on the basis of free exchange of goods and with equal sharing of the savings realized. There was no selfishness and greed here and, consequently, there were no international complications.

Before the war it was estimated by the International Cooperative Alliance that co-operative world trade totaled twenty billion dollars a year. The International Cooperative Wholesale Society combined co-operative wholesales in twenty different countries. Britain and America served co-operative tea from Ceylon. The British soap monopolies were challenged by co-ops soap from eastern Africa. Because there were several "profits" between the farm and the bread on the American table, wheat from our western plains and Canada was shipped and processed by English and Scottish co-op societies and cost less in the British Isles than it did in America.

Co-op stores in Scotland, Belgium, France, Rumania, and Estonia sold co-op oil from Kansas to their members. The Scottish co-op societies owned shares of stock in the North Kansas City, Missouri co-op compounding plant. The "profits" or savings on these transactions were shared alike by consumers in Kansas or Glasgow.

In his book, *The People's Business,* Joshua Bolles sums up this picture by saying:

Here is the key to international co-operative commerce. Here is foreign trade without profit taking. Co-operative trade among the nations eliminates the necessity for wars over markets or sources of raw materials which have been economic factors for centuries in precipitating war.

Not until the economic causes of war, whether between individuals or between nations, are eliminated will we finally build a peaceful world. In co-operation there is an economic foundation for world peace, a blueprint of the future, not a program for Utopia. Co-operation is a form of business enterprise, a way of life that is in operation from day to day with implications that are world-wide.

Thus, I maintain, that co-operation, like power, is a word to conjure with. Quite apart from its religious and metaphysical implications, co-operation is a force of vast potency in our world. There may be those who care nought for religion and for matters which they contemptuously declare belong to the spirit; there may be those who see no meaning in the good as an ethical value; very well, for their benefit, we will divest co-operation of all such connotations, and rest it solely upon the hard ground of economic fact. Even then, we can argue with as much conviction as before. Believe, if you must, in the co-operative system for the single reason that it is good business. Men produce more food, construct more machines, create more wealth when they work co-operatively than when they toil each for his own self-interest. One may or may not believe it to be the will of God; one may or may not care aught about the will of God; but one must submit to scientific fact. And in this restricted field, co-operation is the formula for inheriting the earth.

Many among us distrust religion because of their notion that religion is unworldly, impractical, irrelevant, futile. People who are interested in God cannot be interested in anything else. The followers of Jesus may inherit the sky; but the sky seems a long way off and does not appear to contain much of value anyway. As for us, they say, we who are strong, dynamic and resolute, we shall inherit the earth. It is the earth we want. But what said Jesus? He said something, too, about inheriting the earth. In fact he gave a recipe for so doing. "Blessed are the meek," he proclaimed, "for they shall inherit the earth." The dispute is on a clear question of fact; and there should be a way to adjudicate it on the basis of factual evidence. Who shall inherit the earth? Meekness is at present in sore disrepute. The demand is for strength and courage; obviously qualities diametrically opposed to meekness; we must fight for our rights. Our soldiers must become as hard and brutal as our enemies. They must be taught how to gouge out eyes, to break bones or to torture the foe. This is no time to hear of "turning the other cheek." It is upon the Commandos, the Marines, our unconquerable fighting men we have to depend. Everyone—be he soldier, laborer, businessman or civilian—must take up his position behind the guns. Meekness surely is out of style. All the earth the meek shall inherit is enough to get buried in.

Hitler and his puppets too, have laughed at the idea of meekness! What scorn they have volleyed upon Christianity! It is soft. It is feminine. It is puerile. Christ is a myth and a Jewish lie. Christianity and all its tenets must be cast off and abandoned. The New Order calls for men of iron will. Brotherhood, nonsense! There is one superior race; one people destined to rule the world, to inherit the earth. The earth must submit to its masters, to their ruthless power and might; to the *blitzkrieg*, the concentration camp, the slaughter of hostages. Benighted Christian nations are but easy prey for the Nordic beast. The meek are tender, fit only to be devoured by the German lion.

Meekness, perhaps, is a soft, puerile, feminine word. In fact, all the words in the Sermon on the Mount are the same. The poor in spirit, they that mourn, the righteous, the merciful, the pure in heart, the peacemakers; what avail such specimens today? We, though the sworn adversaries of crude force and the doctrine of might, are inclined to agree. Meekness is no popular gospel among us. We, too, cry for the spirit of iron and of endurance. We, too, must not mourn; the son lost in battle dies for the glory of the fatherland; the child mutilated by the bomb, is only another reason for hatred and determination. Let us learn to hate, however dreadful be the lesson. Who are righteous, except those who go out to give up their lives for their country? Mercy? We receive no mercy at the hands of our enemies. Thus we can give no quarter in return. Ruthlessness and slaughter must be our cry. For every bomb that is dropped upon our cities we must repay with ten dropped upon their cities. The enemy must be wiped from the face of the earth. Whose heart dares to be pure these days? Our softness, our real trouble. We must get hard. Our boys are too idealistic. We must take idealism out of them. They cannot take ideals to war. Peacemakers? What a misled group they are. Who can make peace with a dictator? Peacemakers should be put behind bars. It is not peace that we want, but a sword!

One wonders sometimes, when the boastful, the "mighty" are talking, which country has done best at giving up Christianity, which peoples are the most ruthless. There is so much overlapping and agreement among us all. Jesus was a meek and therefore a weak man. So many times artists depict him with a feminine, holy face with a halo around his head. The sadness and the suffering in his eyes suggest a mourner rather than a living, active leader. Jesus Christ, himself, was too much of an introvert, some say, while others want him to be that way. He is acceptable as a certain type of mystic or visionary, but has nothing to teach real men up against the realities and the struggles of life. Jesus never really did anything; we, on the other hand, are superintendents, bosses, colonels, captains, masters and mates. Our destiny is to rule. We cannot creep and crawl in the attitude of slaves. We are the great and the free; do not talk to us of meekness. Certainly we want to hear nothing so soft as those words in the Beatitude. We repudiate meekness. We repudiate Jesus save for pious Sunday exercises. We shall inherit the earth.

Let us not be so sure. Have we understood Jesus? Or has he been misunderstood, misinterpreted by both preacher and artist down through the years. True, Jesus was meek, but to be truly meek may be the hardest task of a Christian, not a mere retreat and failure to act at all. Jesus said, "Blessed are the meek: for they shall inherit the earth." What could he have meant by such a promise? Can we find any justification for such a bold, sweeping judgment? Possibly Jesus may have been right that the meek "shall inherit the earth." Certainly nobody else seems to be doing it. Perhaps Jesus did know what he was talking about. Perhaps we would do well to listen before total catastrophe has overtaken us and there is nothing left to inherit.

Let us look at Jesus himself. There was nothing weak or indecisive about him. He went through fasting and temptation and came out victorious. The elders in the temple "were astonished at his understanding and answers." The people queried, "What manner of man is this, that even the wind and the sea obey Him?" He talked to them "as one having authority." "From that day forth neither durst any man ask him any more questions." Jesus was a leader of the greatest strength and stature. His glance pierced to the very soul of Pilate. His speech confounded the most astute and learned lawyers of his day. Thousands followed him that they might touch even the hem of his garment. He said, "Follow me," and they who heard gave up all, dropped their nets, left their business, forsook their homes to follow him. Strong will, courage, determination, purpose, directness, power, might, were all his and yet he was at the same time simple and humble. He was a leader, a king, though He had no home nor place to lay his head. Where did his power, this command over other men come from? What was the source of his authority?

If there be anything plain in the gospel of Jesus it is what He meant by meekness and the marvelous way he lived it in his own life. Meekness had within it the entire content of unselfishness, of selflessness, as these qualities were exhibited in his own career. Meekness included giving up for others, control over self, over anger. A complete lack of covetousness, of jealousy, of greed, was inherent in this comprehensive virtue. The positive side of giving up for others, of losing one's soul and yet gaining the whole world, is the basis of the real power that inheres in meekness. Who is able to follow Jesus in exemplifying the real meaning of this word? I say again, to be meek is the hardest duty imposed upon a Christian or the world.

Men of meekness always have been, are today and always will be those with the greatest power in the world. Nehru says in his autobiography, *Toward freedom*, that he is not a religious man, but his behavior proves him to be most deeply religious in the true sense of the term. Though he is writing in prison, there is not a hint of vindictiveness, of vituperation against his accusers or his guards. He has given up deliberately the dearest things in life, wealth, his wife, his daughters, his mother, his father, his friends, for the sake of the cause. He could have traveled in luxury through Europe and America. He could have lived in the high mountains and the cool of his native land with servants attending him. His ability, his keenness, his sense of leadership would have given him power and ever more wealth. But Nehru felt the call of the abject, poverty-stricken, hungry masses of India. He suffered the heat and dust of the countryside to mingle with them and befriend them. He fights their battle, he argues their case, not his own. He has given up self until he has made of India a new and a greater self. Probably the most memorable passage in the book is the story of how he stood with clenched fist, with fingernails piercing his own flesh, and watched policemen strike his aged mother with their lathees until she fell by the roadside with an open wound, her blood mingling with the dust, then with bowed head bore the blows as they descended upon his own back until he too was knocked to earth. His words of comment were these: "Our volunteers gathered together again, many of them bleeding and with split skulls. . . . The bodily pain I felt was quite forgotten in a feeling of exhilaration that I was physically strong enough to face and bear lathee blows."[12] Truly, the reason we repudiate meekness is that we know so little about it, see so little of it.

Fanatical, we may say. No, it was a kind of power and force, the operation of a higher law than the law of brute force exhibited by the police over unarmed and nonviolent natives. How much more strength and resolution it took to stand there, meek and totally poised, than to have struck back. What a contrast with the moral poverty of the police, armed with lathees and mounted upon horses, rising in their stirrups to beat their defenceless foes. On the one side was meekness; on the other was brute force. Where lies the real power, in the army or in the single man? Even England suspects that it is in Nehru. He can keep a whole

[12] *Toward Freedom*, Jawaharlal Nehru, The John Day Co., New York, p. 133.

army at bay, a whole nation wondering what retaliation to adopt next. The power is his.

If ever there existed an example of the authority of passive resistance and meekness, it is found in Gandhi. Sitting there with his thin body wrapped in merely a loincloth, his eyes sunken, his speech soft, he appears to be futile, without influence or effect. Yet who of the 380,-000,000 in India is called first to London or to Delhi? Who has more power? Who is the British lion more afraid of than this meek little man? English imperialists have no illusion as to what the struggle is about. It is not for visions and ideals they are fighting: it is a conflict to determine who shall inherit the earth.

I know another who is meek. I have spoken of him often. He gave up life, health, his all for others. He went into the slums and lived with murderers, harlots, seducers, amid all the filth, vermin and ugliness of their sordid, unholy life. Yet I see that man standing on a bridgehead, alone. In front of him are thousands of workers, goaded on by cries of anarchism and destruction. They carry stones, knives, torches. They are bent on burning down and utterly destroying the factories across that bridge. Behind him, as he stands there alone, are police and soldiers. They have guns leveled and bayonets fixed. It is brute force against wild and uncontrolled anger this time. But no, Kagawa raises his hand. He speaks, he reasons with the crowd. He stands there with nothing but a Bible in his hand, but with utter fearlessness and a piercing tone of command in his voice; his body, his soul, pitted against that wild, uncontrolled mob. The leaders lower their torches, they drop their stones, they return their knives to the sheaths. Finally, silence pervades the crowd. They turn about and straggle back home. Wherein lay the might, that day? Who got things done? Kagawa conquered and preserved what the army could have but conquered and destroyed.

Another man who was meek, I worship. He left his home, his mother, his sisters and brothers. He walked quietly through the countryside. He sat in boats or upon a rock on the hillside as he talked to the people. He told them they must turn the other cheek, go the other mile. Yes, they must forsake everything for others. He himself answered not his accusers. He bowed his head as the soldiers struck him and spat upon him. He looked in prayer to his Father as a crown of thorns was pressed cruelly into his flesh. He never winced as the nails of the cross were driven into his hands and feet. Meekness, ignominy, defeat? No. He conquered life. He gained his soul. He overcame the world.

Do we worship Genghis Kahn, do we worship Caesar, Alexander the Great, Napoleon? They, too, were conquerors. They spread the world out at their feet. Why not worship them? Where are they today? Where are the kingdoms they built? Their empires have long since crumbled to dust. Men cringe at the mention of their names, but hate all they represented. Humanity prays to be delivered from their return, from their example. Their names have become anathema throughout the world, a symbol for all that is wicked.

These men have lost their souls. Jesus in finding his, gained the whole world with it. This is clearly put in the play, "The Terrible Meek," by Charles Rann Kennedy, as the captain of the centurion's guard speaks to Mary after Jesus' death on the cross:

I tell you, woman, this dead son of yours, disfigured, shamed, spat upon, has built a kingdom this day that can never die. The living glory of him rules it. The earth is his and he made it. He and his brothers have been moulding and making it through the long ages; they are the only ones who ever possess it; not the proud: not the idle, not the wealthy, not the vaunting empires of the world. Something has happened up here on this hill today to shake all our kingdoms of blood and fear to the dust. The earth is his, the earth is theirs, and they made it. The meek, the terrible meek, the fierce, agonizing meek, are about to enter into their inheritance.

Meekness is the distinctive, the characteristic Christian virtue. But Christianity is difficult, and meekness cannot be expected to come easily. Which is the easier: is it easier to dominate a man or to be a brother to him? Is it easier to control and monopolize, or to co-operate and divide? Is it easier to hold out to the bitter end, or to confess a mistake? Is it easier to condemn or to forgive? To dominate, to control, to monopolize, these are greed, these are might. They are easy things to do. Their opposites, though difficult, constitute meekness. The meek path is hard to follow; so hard that it takes considerable virtue even to admit that it is a real path. That is why we like to repudiate meekness before we have tried it. It requires a measure of meekness just to admit that meekness is not folly.

We aspire after peace, we yearn for peace, yet we dismiss as impractical and unworthy the only method that can possibly secure it. We want peace, but we do not want it hard enough to adopt the hard way to obtain it. For Jesus, in commanding his followers to be meek, was merely telling them how they might be blessed and happy; he was telling them as well how they might possess the earth. And he was describing to the world what the meek shall finally possess: it will be a world of peace. And it will be a world whose people shall find in good will and in the purpose to co-operate a motive power to sustain its manifold activities. It was no ideal world Jesus was depicting; this was no vision of what might be. The world he was speaking of was this sorry planet now devastated and drenched in blood. The egoists, the advocates of greed and strife and war, they are the visionaries, they are the impractical teachers, though they be schooled in psychology and economics. For their doctrine is false and their schools are asylums for wild men. Of the laws of this universe they know not an element. And in striving to gain the possession of others, they lose even their own. Do we really aspire to possess the world, to inherit the earth? The formula has been delivered.

5

Co-operation or Chaos

THESE LAWS OF THE MORAL AND SPIRITUAL
life have all the characteristics of physical law. There
is one difference, however: their results are slow in appear-
ing, the compass between cause and effect is wide, and the
penalties, though inevitable, are delayed, creating the false
sense that moral law can be violated with impunity. If
one eats tainted food, one feels the effects thereof before
many hours have passed. Thus even primitive men, without
highly developed intellectual faculties or a broad fund of
information upon which to base scientific judgment, soon
become wise in this respect. Since there was a close temporal
connection between eating and suffering, a commandment
forbidding it was not necessary, for the precept received
frank acceptance, save by the incurably stupid, and was
co-operatively acted upon.

The essential difference between moral law and physical
law, and the only real basis for their separation, lies in the
fact that there is a great time interval between act and
consequence in the former. That thou shalt not jump from
a treetop else thou break thy neck, is so obviously true that
the commandment did not need to be inserted in the
Decalogue: everybody knew that. Moral law, however, is
required where only the few with wisdom and experience
realize the ultimate effect of human motives and conduct.
Most of mankind possess but limited mental powers and

are therefore unable of themselves to grasp and to appreciate the full significance of their acts. If this liability be coupled with a refusal to listen to anyone who knows more about this world than they do, then that state of affairs is generated which we behold today.

The ordinary specimen of our race is perfectly certain that he can pursue his own self-interest and attain thereby not only his individual success, but incidentally make his contribution to society. When Jesus tells him he is wrong, that to save his own life he must lose it, he thinks Jesus is wrong, that Jesus is talking about a world of fancy. This individualist and profit-motive advocate has seen a deal of the world with his own eyes, he can give you a host of illustrations of the most ruthless exploiters who are as well great benefactors of humanity, generous supporters of the Church, illustrious names in the annals of mankind. It works, he asserts. But does it? The question is solely one of fact. The dilemma, co-operation or chaos, is not a choice between a world of ideals and a world of fact. It is the alternative between a world of fact, where moral law is an essential ingredient of it, or no world at all. Among men and nations all seeking their own self-interest, there can be no peace; among men and nations seeking their own self-interest, war must eventuate, and amid this war all possessions, the goal of separate self-interests will be lost and annihilated: this is a moral law. Is it true? You think not? Then wait and see. If the great mass of mankind persist in remaining stiff-necked and hardhearted, then the human race is destined to perish from this planet, in the not-too-distant future. God can get along without man, very likely, and on the day of the mutual suicide of the last survivors it will be as true as on the day when the first man was created in His image, that God is love.

Sin might be defined as that type of wrongdoing and
wrong willing where a penalty does not immediately ensue,
where no harm appears to have been done. It is not clear
that one man's trick to take advantage of a competitor has
any other effect than to sharpen the latter's wits, which is a
good thing for him. It is not clear that your or my way
of doing business within our own tiny spheres has anything
to do with such a holocaust as the World War. But it has,
though we cannot see it: it is a truth though we cannot
grasp it. There is no essential difference between war and
what we are wont to call peace. Our peace is no real peace,
but a state of suspended military operations. The motives,
the ambitions, the satisfactions which sustain us in time of
war are precisely those which activated us in the interim
of peace. War and peace are cut of the same cloth. Is there
any essential difference between the notes our State Department addressed to Japan in the latter months of 1941
and what the Japanese did to us at Pearl Harbor? Is there
any essential difference between protecting or extending
one's possessions by force or by the threat of force? There
is no problem of war, for religion to address itself to: there
is the single problem of war and peace: the problem of co-
operation or chaos. All war does is to hold a mirror before
our faces and show us the sort of people we really are,
and if we do not like what the mirror shows us we are, it
will accomplish nothing to break the mirror. We, who
make war, whose so-called peaceful way of life can issue
in naught but war, we must be transformed. We must
be remade, we must be born again. We must find new
motives for our living. We must co-operate; then there will
be no problem of war, for we will be peaceful men, not
peace-wishing men. The problem of war, and peace of the
1918-1939 type as the alternative, is a wholly fictitious

problem—the six of one and half a dozen of the other sort of choice. The real choice is between co-operation and chaos.

No, I am not inveighing against this particular war, even though every one of us who has thought at all and who has any sense of the horror of it all has yearned that he might plunge into the center of the inferno and raise his hands to heaven, imploring God to strike all of us dead rather than suffer it to go on. We have seen, however, that man is free and God will not stop it. Jesus stands there, but men close their eyes and their ears and blaspheme with their mouths and then push Christ aside to clear the way to their goal of annihilation and victory. There is no possibility of halting it now. The avalanche is rolling down the mountainside and one would be crushed to earth in struggling to stem it. Those who have defied the unconquerable, however much they have lost, have not lost their souls: the bishops of Norway, the Niemoellers, all of those, rotting in jails, and in concentration camps, roaming the world as refugees or suffering the ignominy of objectors, the hostages and the Mayor Ordens who have sacrificed their lives. These have not bowed the head, nor bent the knee. Verily, they shall have their reward. To them be the everlasting tribute of free men.

Or shall we simply forget them? Shall we go on with our nefarious business of competition, monopoly, rivalry, slavery and dominance? Can we keep all this horror, this blood, this destruction before our eyes long enough to make a peace of brotherhood and good will which will end forever this carnage and hell? It is the question of co-operation or chaos, co-operation or slavery for the white race. Chaos it will be if we refuse to put on "sackcloth and ashes," to beat our breasts and without even so much as daring to raise our eyes to heaven, implore that God be merciful unto us sinners. We must repent. We must find the new life for every collapse of the old will be worse confounded.

These are religious phrases, you say, the language of the Bible. There is no time for Bible reading now for we are practical men in the midst of war and are bending every effort to win. My answer is that it is because I am convinced we are near the actual winning of this war—that is, the military phase of it—that I am overwhelmingly concerned that we begin to think beyond that point to the much more potentially important phase we will enter, after an armistice is wrung from a defeated enemy.

That will be the true crisis. A decision will have to be rendered then. Armistice Day is a day of choice, and no emotional orgy after the pattern of November 11, 1918, can keep it from being such. That former debauch indeed signalized, by its very lack of restraint and unbridled self-gratification, that we did then and there choose and that we chose wrongly and wickedly. Not even the most thoroughgoing advocate of freedom would contend that a genuine choice lies before either a man or nation at every moment of existence. On rare occasions the dilemma is presented to us: if God be God, serve Him; if Baal be God, serve him. But between these peaks of choice stretch long tedious valleys to be traversed, through which we must plod, inexorably following the course we have set our feet upon. December 7, 1941, was no day of national choice: that was a day of fate. We discovered then where we had been traveling through the years. At Pearl Harbor there was no turning back. Pearl Harbor was destined to happen. We had willed it that way long ago. True, at that juncture there was a slight bend in the road. The landscape beyond the bend was just a bit novel, perhaps, and we had expected to behold past the turn a slightly more familiar sight. But still the road was old, and the change was not so startling that we could not adapt ourselves to the scenery almost overnight. As a nation we rather welcomed war. But nobody who has ever experienced the authentic sense of choice, could mistake that enthusiasm for freedom. Today and tomorrow, as long as the fighting lasts, it is idle to boast that we are free. We are committed to Baal, we are serving out a vow we once made to Mammon. But the day will come when once more, for an hour, for a moment, somewhere, someone is free to speak for you and me and for us all. It is that day we should be looking forward to and preparing for.

If God be God, serve Him. If Baal be God, serve him. It is either human brotherhood or a world where our children will live in continuous war, abject fear and eventual chaos. The situation may be summarized in the words of the Earl of Athlone speaking from Toronto on June 22, 1942:

This is a revoluntionary war, and a revolutionary peace will be by no means incompatible. This war . . . is a phase in a world revolution. The war of 1914-1918 was the first phase. It accomplished nothing and so this second war was inevitable. A third upheaval is likely unless the peace is revolutionary. We must place greater emphasis on the things of the spirit and less on material wealth. We must see that our economic system is adjusted to the requirements of the consumer rather than the requirements of the producer, and we must see that our social services produce an increasingly high minimum standard of living throughout the world.

Thus this British peer puts the choice clearly before us. Our choice is more acute and imperative than any the world has ever before faced. We can continue the old system, have our pound of flesh, and a peace hatched out by the politicians. We can set up again areas of control and mandates. We can continue to have a "high standard of living," which is average and not actual, for England and America, while India, the natives in Africa, the Chinese, the Japanese, two-thirds of the human race, live in cruel poverty and actual starvation of body and soul. Or we can establish an era of brotherhood, of racial equality and equal opportunity where co-operation will be the co-ordinating and integrating power. We can institute free trade between nations with common access to raw materials, whereby the standard of living for the whole world can be gradually raised, with the money we would otherwise waste on war and competition. We can establish a federation of nations which will be a real government with powers and rights granted by sovereign states. This will involve religious, social, economic and political co-operation. But the peace so wrought will be just and durable. Any other kind of peace will make necessary future wars, more horrible and devastating than our present holocaust, and ultimately will lead to world-wide chaos. Is it for that that God has given man freedom? Man's freedom cannot and shall not terminate that way. We, the common people, must rise up and assert our rights. If we alone are free to decide, we must resolve to make the decision.

Let us face the issue a little more squarely. I have said that the world has never so faced this alternative before. What about the last World War? Did we not face it then? Not surely in the same way we are facing it now. A glance at any world map will show what I mean. The last war was confined to a comparatively small section of Europe. True, nearly all nations were involved in it. World War I was a tremendous struggle and cost billions of dollars and millions of lives. But the geography of the present war is far more inclusive. All of Europe has been drawn into the vortex—Scandinavia, Russia from Moscow to the Caucasus, the British Isles have been cruelly bombed. If there ever was such a thing as total warfare, Europe has at last known it. Only five small countries, the Irish Free State, Sweden, Portugal, Spain and hardy Switzerland have in some miraculous manner kept out of the actual shooting, though they have been involved in many terrible respects. But that is only the beginning. Africa has been ravaged by the campaigns in the desert, the fight for Suez, for Italian Somaliland and Ethiopia, and in free French territory: that continent is an armed camp to its very tip at Capetown. Turning to Asia, there is China prone and ravaged, yet an unbelievable bulwark of defense, Siam, Malaya, Burma, Singapore, India, Iraq and Iran, the islands of the sea, great and small, and finally Australia, all in the thick of the combat. What is left at peace in the world? There are Siberia and North and South America. But Siberia is an armed camp and the wail of refugees sent to the vast reaches of steppe and plain from Poland and the small states bordering Russia, rises day and night. America has escaped in a sense, but if one takes a trip by ship down the east coast one sees the burned hulks of freighters or tankers or the masts just visible above the tops of the waves. The desolation of war has left scarcely a spot on earth untouched. And in the next war, if there be one, America will be as vulnerable as England has been in this war. Has there ever been such a world crisis before? We shut our eyes and clench our fists and from the very depths of our soul cry out to God that it must not happen again. Whether our prayer be answered or not, this is the choice precisely before us. God cannot save us if we insist on damning ourselves.

The Church is frequently accused these war days of being in the war with only half a heart. The tough-minded and self-styled practical businessmen tell us occasionally we churchmen are interested in peace. This accusation need not be answered, for it is admitted. But let us who are the Church referred to, get tough in our own defense. Let us reply in this wise: Yes, we are interested in peace. We are working for peace as a practical matter. Let me ask you this. You are a "hardheaded" businessman. You see and think clearly. Is the sole end of all your long hours, your worry and struggle with prices, with priorities, with labor, to be paying the tax bill the government presents for the support of war? During the next twenty-five years are you going to give the best of your life, build up another reserve and then just before you die see it all taken again for another war? Is that the end of life in this world for you, a leading businessman, just to work and slave and build up wealth that it may be later blown to pieces and your own children, your own grandchildren, blown to pieces with it? As a practical man, there should be nothing you are more interested in than the question of peace. It is more realistically significant today from just the dollar-and-cents standpoint than any other question which you could possibly face.

Yes, leaving aside all other issues and their just and crying claims, from merely a hard cash point of view, every businessman should be vitally interested in the maintenance of peace. The trouble is that the fight with Washington to get material to keep the factory running is at the moment the biggest problem on their hands. The bogey of Hitler or the Yellow Peril, realistic and actual as it has been and is, has kept us awake at night. We never stop to realize, that the government's system of priorities has developed, that Hitler has sprung to life, that the Yellow Peril hangs over our heads, just because we have heretofore refused to face the real issue. The businessman, the banker, the industrialist, the commercial magnate, should lead the peace movement, if for no other reason than economic considerations.

Years ago, Stanley Jones wrote a most prophetic book entitled *The Choice Before Us*. For chapter after chapter, he argued that it was a choice of either Christ and his program of brotherhood and co-operation, or the alternative of world revolution. In his closing paragraphs, after challenging the businessman to action, he uttered these most significant words: "When the revolution comes and the catastrophe is upon us, the only answer history can give is 'they were not big enough.'" That was written before the present debacle. The revolution has since come. But the question still remains, "Are they big enough?" Big enough to learn a little?

Let us listen to a college professor, James Burnham, of New York University, in his book *The Managerial Revolution*, written at the beginning of the war. This is a disclosure from a genuine business economist. "Managerial government" means socialist government with society having little to do with it. The main contention of the book is that business and industry have failed to manage themselves. They have renounced their former autonomy and are more and more inviting the power of government to manage their affairs. Thus is generated a species of government control perilously near to Fascism. Not only has business failed to order its own house, however, but government itself also has lost its powers to govern. Great Britain was lost, according to Burnham, at the defeat of France (that was before Egypt, Singapore and the flare-up of internal conflicts) and the Empire is bound to disintegrate. Smaller nations have degenerated to the point where they are absolutely dependent upon the larger nations. Thus the governments themselves, once they have taken over the business activities of nations, will seek succor under the wings of the larger, stronger powers. This will result in vast coalitions of nations in managerial areas. There will be one in North and South America, including Canada and Australia, with the United States, of course, as the central power. In Europe will center another coalition, whose head Burnham predicted would be Germany. It now appears more likely to be Russia, or Russia and England, for the latter is certainly still in the picture. For a third area, he marked out Asia with Japan (more probably, he would now say, China) as the sovereign state. However we construe all this, the scheme is not at all impossible. In fact, it sounds only too prophetic if true world federation is not consummated. The end envisioned by Burnham is these super politico-economic entities vying with one another for world markets and raw materials. What a vision! What a perfect setup for the next world war!

Exactly that will eventuate and take shape if another principle is not applied. The world therein forecast reduces us all to slavery; to the slavery of preparing for future war; in fact, to the slavery of perpetual conflict, for we have learned that the last war never ceased and the present war is only a continuation of a perennial combat. This slavery means fear, the fear of insecurity, the fear of attack, the pressure of building larger and larger armaments, the erecting of forts and barriers all over the country, the building of bombproof shelters in mountains and hills and under cities, the control of business and profits for taxation, which in an incessant stream pours into armament production and war preparation; together with trade barriers, international distrust, exclusion acts and the motley crew of aggressions and provocations. Slavery? How serene the life of the slave relative to the mental strain and cruel fears rampant in such a world.

But that is not all. There is the genuine prospect that our sons and daughters may become the actual slaves of the yellow and brown races. We in the West cannot easily appreciate the growing vitality, the pace of change, the quickening life of China and the seething unrest in India. It should be everyone's concern to read Edgar Snow's *Battle for Asia* or Madame Chiang Kai-shek's *China will Rise Again*. The Japanese have always had ambitions for world conquest and ideas of oriental superiority. This conception, largely borrowed from China, with a dose of good Western imperialism, is the basis of the present Japanese belief in her ability to rule the world. Put these three great nations together, China, India and Japan, add a hostile native Africa and a neutral Russia, and where would the white race be? This is not a bogey I am trying to conjure up. I am simply recording the fact of the way a billion people, two-thirds of the human race, with vast resources and absolutely unlimited man power, feel about white supremacy. Where would the white race be on the basis of actual brute power, save in subjection?

I recently talked with a doctor who had practiced in India for five years. He wanted to stay there. He was offered a practice as surgeon with a most eminent Indian physician who controlled a private hospital and who had a large clientele. All agreements were made and papers drawn up. Two months before the plan was to go into effect, the Indian doctor had to come to his American friend and said to him, "I am extremely chagrined and truly perturbed but we shall have to cancel our arrangements. It would not be practical or even safe for a white man to settle down in India right now." Other such stories could be told of the Japanese, and even the Chinese have their fingers crossed. They are watchfully waiting to see what our next move will be. And, I am afraid, they are resolved to be governed accordingly.

Such feeling and resentment in India is growing, and will increase until Indians have been given equality (they will some day get their freedom), until brotherhood and co-operation displace greed and avarice. Pearl Buck has repeatedly told us this. She said it at the East and West Association meeting in the spring of 1942 when she boldly declared:

Thus India, when she is politically freed, must remove the great human inequalities among her people and establish freedom for all if she is to assume her proper place in the new world. We Americans have exactly the same task as India. Our people have political freedom, but not human equality. Our Civil War rid us of the slave system, but it did not give the freed human equality. The people of China have human equality but not political equality.

We are all partial democracies, and we cannot be sure of victory until we are made whole. But what a great struggle is ours, the most ennobling that the human mind has ever conceived, that people must be free. And if they are to be free as human beings they must be equal.

Francis B. Sayre utters the same sentiment:

If democracy means anything it means equality of opportunity. Faith in democracy, the American faith, means equality of opportunity extended to all peoples, to all races, to all creeds, to all classes. It is an all-embracing faith and it extends into the political sphere, the economic sphere, the social sphere and the spiritual sphere of life.

Unless granted that equal opportunity as a matter of justice, the yellow man and the brown man are going to demand and get it for themselves. We already know only too well how they fight. If we do not find a way to peace, brotherhood and co-operation, these hordes will be on our doorstep even as the savage tribes of the North knocked at the portals of Rome and finally sacked the city. Did the patricians in the time of Caesar ever think that some day their sons and daughters would be taken prisoners by the sons and daughters of the very prisoners who were then their slaves? One would have been laughed to scorn who mentioned such a remote possibility. When we are considering our own future, let us keep one eye on history, the other on geography. We do not care to prejudge which would be worse,—German slavery or Asiatic domination. Both dire contingencies must be forestalled by the same means: a peace of justice and co-operation.

It is as simple as that: a peace of justice and co-operation! But how hard it comes; how high the price. It is really the hardest course possible. Peace requires self-control, it takes sacrifice, it means actually giving up for the benefit of all. Yet it pays. In fact, peace is the only course that will pay. We are faced with a tremendous choice: co-operation or chaos.

Down in Mexico is a huge co-operative printing plant which does all the government printing. The front entrance opens upon a beautiful white marble and pressed rock winding staircase leading to the third story of the building. As one climbs toward the top at the crown of the staircase and directly in the center of the spacious upper hall rests a massive piece of statuary. Its shape and form seem to overwhelm one, as one comes nearer to gaze upon it. Then its bold outline is fully grasped. It is a huge tank with guns blazing. Behind it, urging it forward, are militarists and dictators and a various assortment of their species. Opposing soldiers are crushed by it, but the workers and the common people of the world are standing shoulder to shoulder against it. In fact, they have all but pushed it over. One more great heave and the tank will have fallen back on the militarists and demagogues frantically pushing it on.

It may be that the common people, those who have suffered so much in this war, the mothers, the sons, the wives, the children of civilians, factory workers and soldiers alike, it may be that these are the ones to blaze the path to co-operation and to overthrow the monster, war. I feel ever confident of this, as I see the common people in the field or in the factory, at home or abroad, wherever they are. In them I think I discern the spirit of brotherhood, the spirit of co-operation, the will to peace. For they are peaceful when given scope to be so. They—we—the common people, should decide this peace. We may do so if we will. For where a duty lies, there resides the power to fulfill it. We are not the ones proposing the issue, co-operation or chaos. God has done that. We are not demanding the decision. God is demanding that. But we must decide, we must answer, we must choose. Let none other do it for us, in our name; unless his reply is our own.

But how, one asks, both in hope and out of desperation, can this good will, latent in the hearts of millions, find expression? What organ shall articulate and render vocal the aspirations of masses of men, devoted to peace and peaceful pursuits? By what instrument or device are ideals to be made effective and potent? How is God to function in the affairs of men? I have endeavored to prolong the interrogation to the point where you will cry out the answer which to me seems so obvious. The church is the answer. How save through the Church can the will of God be affirmed? What institution save the Church exists upon earth for no other purpose than to embody and to realize this spirit of co-operation, that alone can rescue us from chaos.

Our conception, our definition of the Church, states just that: the Church is the organization whose primary purpose is to establish co-operation and to render love operative. We must, in times like these, search for foundations. Much of the superstructure of the Church has been bombed out; much ecclesiastical architecture has been reduced to rubble. The stained glass of theological speculations, the gargoyles and trimmings, the ornate luxuries of doctrine and dogma, have collapsed in the general crash. What will survive of the Church is that part of it that is essential, those elements that live deep within the hearts of men and in the eternal truth of the Gospel. This is the seed that shall outlive the storm and the blast, and that shall grow anew. The Church in the coming day must be a new growth, though its roots be sunk deep in the heritage of the past. The Church has the answer, our answer, yet it must seek it amid the ruins of itself. When I speak, therefore, of the Church, I am not referring to ministers and priests, ruling boards or bodies, its "political" or business aspects. These are important, of course, in patent respects indispensable, and one marvels at the power of vast world organizations of individual churches and faiths. But the real thing we are talking about is the Church in its relation to people; how it is really going to help people to live; how it is to change lives and to transform the world.

What is meant, can be brought out by an anecdote. During the visit of Kagawa to America in 1936, he was spending some time in New York. I was eager to show him the sights. I asked him if he would not like to see the Cathedral of St. John the Divine. That was the biggest thing just then in the religious life of the city. His answer was unforgettable: "I am not interested in stone and great building. I am interested only in what church is doing for people."

It is the Church in action with people that we are talking about. How much do we believe in that Church? "Upon this rock I will build my church; and the gates of hell shall not prevail against it." If this voice fails us, we must be prepared for the total silence of death.

Today, however, it does seem that the gates of hell are prevailing. War, destruction and all the hell of bombings, submarine and tank, all the horrible atrocities upon countless millions of innocent people have all but annihilated the Church in certain places. The actual teaching of atheism, derision the Church is assailed by in vast areas of Europe, especially in Germany and Russia, have all but developed an atheistic generation. The Quisling control of the Norwegian bishops, revolutions in Spain or Mexico, the secularism and materialism of our own land, combine to spell doom for the Church. Can the Church survive these onslaughts? Are not the gates of hell prevailing? Do we really care about the Church? Do we dare to hope?

But this is not the first crisis. The Church stood dauntless throughout other dark ages. Barbarian hordes swept down from the North and overran Rome and the great cities of the Empire. Not only the Church, but all culture, education and government were apparently wiped out. The Church was still standing, however, at the end. When the dawn broke again, it revealed a Church that had flourished and grown strong and mighty during the night.

I once visited a church which had withstood all these avalanches. A group of us stood one day in that ancient church at Nuremberg, Germany. The building was over a thousand years old. As we entered, a sense of awe descended upon us. We walked on tiptoe and spoke in whispers. All about us were the graves of great leaders, artists, sculptors, educators, priests belonging to those past thousand years. On the outside, around the building, noble figures of many generations encompassed us. We beheld with wonder the pulpit carved by hand from marble and hardwood, the delicate work of a skilled but nameless craftsman. We examined the baptistry and the beauty of the stained-glass windows. The church has been there for countless years, through numberless perils. It had been for a thousand or more years, the center of the vibrant, busy life of that ancient city. One wonders what is happening in that church today. Will it survive Nazism, the bombings? Is it still intact after the many aerial attacks upon Nuremberg? Yes, that church still stands. Possibly that lovely and beloved edifice will be destroyed, but the Church will remain in the hearts of people who have worshiped there.

The vitality of the Church is amazing. Stories continually reach the World Council of Churches and the Foreign Missionary Conference concerning what is happening in various parts of the world under the stress of persecution and war. In China, people are worshiping in caves, on the sides of mountains, in graveyards. Cemeteries are favored spots because the Japanese do not regard it worth while to bomb them. One informant says, they hold a service wherever a leader can be found. Denominational lines have vanished. Catholic priests are ministering to Protestants and Protestants to Catholics in the stricken and refugee areas. From France come most astounding stories of the purge by fire. Dr. Adolph Keller of Switzerland, Director of the Central Bureau for Inter-Church Aid, affirms that out of France will come a depth of faith and a new inner vision which will revitalize the world Church. The Church is making ready to speak and to proclaim her original message of salvation.

Nothing could be more heartening and fearless than the stand of the Norwegian bishops against the machinations of Quisling. In Germany many thousands are still worshiping in the Confessional Church, the group to which Pastor Niemoeller belongs, and have steadfastly refused to bow to the will of the Hitlerite bishops. Thousands more are worshiping privately though forced to give outward lip service to the new regime.

As sure as the rising of tomorrow's sun, a revival of the inner springs of religious motivation will result from the horror and suffering of this world upheaval. A closer unity is manifest everywhere between Protestant groups and between the Catholic and Protestant clergy. A wider *rapprochement* is developing with the other faiths. A new spirit of understanding and brotherhood is abroad in the world. There stands the Church, precisely there where you see these signs.

The mission centers have contributed a significant and valuable force these latter years! Many reports on China tell of the sacrifice and the heroism of missionaries. Their leadership in the "New China" is undisputed. The government is in charge of the graduates of their schools. Industry is fostered by the technical schools of Christian colleges and agriculture is expanded as a result of the agricultural schools of Christian missions. In its financial statement, the International Missionary Council says:

This report of the financial aid given to sustain the "Orphaned Missions" is evidence that the world-wide fellowship of Christians is being expressed in warm, living, factual realities. . . . Every mission, regardless of nationality or creed, that has been separated by war from its parent church in Europe and has been known to be in distress, has received such help as was needed to maintain all work that was essential to the life of the younger churches.

The only contact with the thousands of war prisoners in the Axis countries is through the Church and the Church agencies. The Y.M.C.A. has recently gained access to the American soldiers in Japan. In many cases the Church is the only contact between different nations in Europe. In Geneva, Switzerland, the World Council of Churches, the Ecumenical Chaplaincy Commission for Prisoners of War and the Central Bureau for Inter-Church Aid are all functioning still and carrying on continuous efforts to aid refugees and prisoners of war. There stands the Church! These, too, are signs of it.

Without question, the Church will emerge from this holocaust with more potential power than she has ever possessed before. The Church and the principles of Christianity indeed are all that will be left to build upon. The Church will be changed, that is certain, but will she be changed enough? If the Church is to embrace her rightful place and fruitful leadership, she must be a different Church. The Church must practice the renunciation she must set about preaching. Nations must give up something of themselves; they must abandon their national sovereignty for the sake of world federation and internationl co-operation. Here lies what is at once the greatest opportunity and the most imperative necessity for the Church to assert her leadership. Can the Church overcome her own selfish and bigoted interests, her narrow traditions, and rise to the heights of genuine brotherhood? The Church must clear her own throat before she answers the question before the world. Let it be in no rasping voice that the church cries, co-operation. Can nations, these worldly and secular units, unite on a basis of authentic peace, when religious groups the world over continue waging war with one another?

One recalls the terrific controversy not so long ago concerning the appointment of the representative to the Vatican by the President of the United States. Even liberal papers were busy fanning the flame of narrow sectarianism. They were putting in the mouths of less liberal groups the very words they might use if they were to withdraw from the Federal Council or even execute a denominational split over the matter. The Catholics were maligned, the President was damned, but no good interest was served. These Protestant groups were hypocritically saying to the nations of the world, "You must get together. You must practice brotherhood. We will give you the fine principles of justice, equality and freedom that you must follow. But we as Church people, oh, no. It is not for us. We must keep our differences. The question of baptism by immersion or by sprinkling is a vital issue. Upon the question of how you define the divinity of Christ depends your entrance into heaven. Catholics must be opposed because we fear their control of government and do not accept their dogmas. Other religions have no rights and must all be converted to our own. No, we cannot possibly give up our pet differences. Does the Church wonder that so many are not disposed to listen?

During preparation for a national religious gathering,

recently, the committee was demanding that the hotels should provide for Negro delegates. Leading church officials were toiling to convince a hotel manager. His reply was, "Yes, gentlemen, we will take in Negroes when you take them into your churches!" To date, the situation has remained stationary. Nobody has made a move. Can anybody make an answer? It is precisely by reason of such indecision, that at the coming peace conference, politicians may assemble and the Church will be left at home, watching a process of brotherhood develop or fail of development, which it cannot direct, because of its own impotence and hesitations. This, let us hope and pray, will not be the case. But to avert this dismal prospect is our united responsibility. That the gates of hell may not prevail against it, imposes a solemn and arduous duty upon us all.

We can rejoice, however, that the great task shows indications of fulfillment. Our faith in the Church is not built on mere ideational fiction. It is based upon actual experience and knowledge. The movement for world-wide Protestant federation is developing fast. Today there are eighty-two Christian bodies which have agreed to join this world organization. In Great Britain the new Council of Churches, including both free church and Anglican bodies, has been consummated and it is functioning most salutarily. The late Dr. William Paton, general secretary of the World Council of Churches, told us on his last visit to America of the "Sword of the Spirit" movement which had come out of the war in England and which was joining Catholic and Protestant bodies in certain common enterprises. In the mission field the new indigenous churches are proclaiming a newly discovered unity. In America the strong Episcopal denomination has now formally joined the Federal Council, Presiding Bishop Henry St. George

Tucker has been elected president, and others who are not now members are working on Formulae for such co-operation. A great national organization is being formulated to bring all the seven national interdenominational bodies into one combined organization. And what is more, we are certainly working together in many new and broader areas of inter-faith co-operation. The present development in this field is nothing less than phenomenal, and a decade ago would have been impossible. Thus faith can be based on facts and the actual present trends.

There is another place, also, where great progress is being made. This is in the field of social and economic programs, in what we have called co-operatives. There is probably no more interesting venture in the Church relating itself to the life of the people than in Nova Scotia. Here race and faith lines are obliterated in one total effort to help people. The priest or minister is out during every day of the week, guiding and aiding his parishioners in solving their food, housing, fishing, farming, credit, medicine problems, as they arise. The Church is identical with the people and the people are identical with the Church. Since the industrial unit is perfectly integrated, it is perforce religious. Father J. J. Tompkins believed in people. He was criticized and disciplined; for eight long years he fought a discouraging but a winning battle. The first co-operative scheme was eventually put into practice. Then it proceeded to spread! Father M. M. Coady could now write a book about Nova Scotia co-operatives, saying the people are "masters of their own destiny," and George Boyle could write another entitled *Democracy's Second Chance*, in which he proved that the "second chance" is working out in Nova Scotia. The Nova Scotia co-operative experiment is religion in action. This is the solution we are searching for and the only solution possible.

I attended Father Tompkins' church one day. What an experience that was! "Catholic formalism"? No. Worship was as vital as any I have ever participated in. I knelt in prayer with miners and steel workers, and the prayer joined in was authentic. There was a relationship between priest and people which was reality itself. A few days later a group of us went to Sunday worship in a little rural church belonging to the United Church of Canada out in the woods of Cape Breton Island. It was a Scottish community with a Scottish preacher. There were one hundred and fifty people present, the entire population, and all the building would hold. Those people knew their minister for they all worked together to earn a common living in that community. The minister rode on the load of flour that they had bought co-operatively, as they proceeded proudly through town. He was the instigator and leader of the credit union. In class discussions and by talking to them out on the farm he was teaching his parishioners how to grow better crops, to co-operate in marketing, and in every way to live one for all and all for one. Religion can be a vital force in human affairs when it is brought within the compass wherein men live. In our own country, Monsignor Luigi Ligutti, secretary of the National Catholic Rural Life Conference, has led in developing a new co-operative housing project in Granger, Iowa. He worked with Catholic and Protestant alike. Little Father Soucey up in Maine has virtually transformed another community, which previous to his labors, was almost hopeless. Cases and illustrations could be multiplied. But I am concerned now only to state and affirm the principle they embody: that co-operation is the love principle in action. Working together is a policy that works.

Too often does the Church insist that her role is to deal only in principles. Their practical application is neither her business nor her prerogative. Too often, as a result, the Church exhausts her efforts in vague generalities which not even she herself takes seriously, or intends to be governed by. Vacuous idealism therefore is the Church's chief peril today, and the danger that she will succumb to it is the greatest peril the world is facing. It is in fields and workshops, on shipboard and in the factory that human problems originate, and here they must be met and solved. It is in this practical field that the choice of co-operation or chaos confronts us. To applaud co-operation and not to strive to make co-operation effective in actual human associations, is to fix our eyes on the stars and fall into the pit. By co-operation therefore, the Church—or whoever else gives the answer—must mean more than a system of ideas. Co-operation means a working together of men and machines, an arrangement of forces. Co-operation means co-operatives. For the gates of hell are very, very real.

6

Man's Dominion Over the World

AN OLD HEBREW SEER ONCE SAT IN FRONT of his tent in communion with his God. The night was clear, starlit and sparkling, one of the nights which are so common in Palestine. He gazed into the heavens, his mind was wrestling with ponderous questions. What was the purpose of man? Why was man created? What was the relation of man to God?

He had sat there many nights before. God had come very close to him. Sometimes he prayed. When an answer seemed to come, and a great thought was revealed, he praised Jehovah God. For hours at a time he would continue in deep and serious communion. The stories his mother had told him about the beginnings of the world and the creation were recalled, reheard by his ears. The experiences of his own life were relived and thought through in every detail.

The fact of God was a positive heritage of his race. Jehovah was the beginning of everything that exists. God as Creator had been an accepted idea for many past generations. God had created the earth, divided the night from the day, made the dry land to appear, God had hung the sun and the moon in the heavens. At that thought this old Israelite would look up at the myriad points of light in the blue above. God seemed to care so much for man that he made the stars also. God had brought into being the fish of the sea and the fowl of the air and every living thing upon the earth. Then God created man. In His own image created He him.

Then one night came the answer to the question. The answer was perfectly clear now. Man was above all else that God had created. He was superior to the fish, the birds, the beasts of the field. The old Hebrew went back in his mind to that experience when he was out on the sea in one of the small boats of his day. A great fish had come up and almost overturned the little craft, but man was to conquer even that monster fish. He was to have dominion over the fish of the sea.

Only yesterday, he remembered, he had watched a great eagle as the giant bird had soared down from a high cliff and swooped low to try to catch one of the little lambs of the flock. He had rushed over and rescued the cringing creature just in time. With a scream at being thus baffled, the eagle had soared to an even higher crag, almost out of sight. Man was destined to control the mighty birds of the air.

Then came the thought of the day when singlehanded, with only the strength of his staff and his sling to depend upon, he had subdued the wild beast which prowled stealthily out of the forest. It was a struggle of skill and intelligence against strength. That combat was conclusive. Man was to have dominion over even the beasts of the field. He summed it all up in his own words this way: "So God created man in His own image . . . and God blessed them, and God said unto them, 'Be fruitful, and multiply, and replenish the earth and subdue it: and have dominion over the fish of the sea, and over the fowl of the air, and over every living thing that moveth upon the earth.'" Man was to have "dominion over every living thing that moveth upon the earth."

Man long since has gained the dominion forecast in the early Scriptures. He has gone far and away beyond any triumph the imagination of that old teacher of Israel could possibly have conjured up. He has taken the fish for food. He has captured the great fish, the whale, for oil and bone. He has tamed the fowl of the air and trained them to do his bidding. The chicken and the duck rejoice in the captivity of his farmyard. The dove carries his messages afar. The trained cormorant fishes for him and the canary entertains him with song. He has taken the beasts of the field and domesticated them; wild cattle to give him milk and meat, the horse to plow his field and to carry him on his journey. The wolf and the wildcat have settled down as his pets and companions. Man has subdued all animal life, and what he could not conquer he has exterminated.

Men has gained dominion over every living thing upon the face of the earth. But man did not stop there; he went on and on. He has climbed into the very air, the sky, the heavens, and has captured the electricity of the lightning flash, harnessed the power of the sun's rays. The ultimate secrets of the universe beyond his sight he is investigating that he may find more power. His planes soar higher and higher through the outermost reaches of the stratosphere. He is setting up a telescope which will bring the moon within twenty-five miles of the earth and which will reveal new worlds, other sources of power, far beyond the now visible space. Man is going on and on in his search for greater dominion over everything upon the face of the earth, below its surface, in the depths of it, above and beyond it, in the vast stretches of space unknown. What vast power man now holds in his hands! What an incredible creature he is! But when we look at the way man is using the power he has gained, we are not so proud of him. For, while these accessions of power make man appear godlike, the ends to which he has used this power scarcely resemble the purposes of God.

One day a group of us were going to Birmingham, Alabama. As the train rolled along, we passed a series of crude, oven-shaped piles of stone. There were dozens of them along the siding. We wondered what they were and finally called the porter. He told us they were the old ovens in which the iron ore used to be smelted when it was first discovered in these hills. Charcoal was used to fire them and the rough pig iron produced was loaded and shipped off to the foundries. But at Birmingham that night we saw the modern equivalent of those ovens, the furnaces where iron is now being refined. What a sight that valley was! The whole sky was a reflection of the belching fire and smoke of the inferno. The great blast furnaces roared their fury. From countless stacks and open pits came the flames of fire, the billowing of smoke and the hissing of steam as the ore was melted and poured. One can visit those plants and see for himself; the huge blast furnaces being tapped and the sparkling, white-hot steel as it flows through the ditch of sand to the immense ladles which carry it to the molds; the heaving pieces of brightly glowing ingots, reheated to white-hot temperature, swung by overhead cranes to the gaping jaws of the rollers; then the flashing back and forth shuttle-wise, of this seething mass until it is rolled into great long car rails or girders for a Golden Gate Bridge, or frames for an Empire State Building! Thus man has gained his dominion over the crude iron ore which was first smelted down in those simple little ovens, and all in such brief time as to make the conquest seem miraculous.

I remember my first trip to New York City. My father took me to see the Flatiron Building at Fifth Avenue and

Twenty-third Street. How dingy and insignificant it looks now. But how imposing it was then! It was the first building to be constructed with steel girders in New York, and people traveled miles just to gaze upon it. But now you can pass a vacant lot in the fall, and by the following spring find that a thirty-five story structure stands on that site. The steel work goes up "overnight." The brick veneer is laid by masons working on three levels. The old Hebrew sages surely underestimated man's capacities, and no seer of a hundred years ago could have had the remotest conception of man's fantastic accomplishments during the century before him. Man merely claps his hands and a bridge is thrown over a river, a building arises fifty, seventy-five stories into the air, tunnels are bored, broad highways are laid down; iron horses speed across the rails; mammoth steel ships ply the ocean; submarines dive into the depths of the sea. The magic lamp of Aladdin would have been impotent to effect the actual happenings man has wrought on the earth. Yet he is not satisfied. Man's appetite is insatiable. There must be stores of power as yet untapped, perhaps unsuspected. Thus man is grappling with this problem of the cosmic rays. Man will go on and on in extending his dominion. He will not rest content until he has subdued every force in this vast universe, from the potential power of the microscopic atom to the cosmic ray streaming from farthest outer space.

There stands man, high on the pedestal he has made for himself, with all the power he controls grasped in his mighty hand. Lightnings of electricity flash from his clenched fist. His arm shakes with the roar of the wheels of his industry. Messages from his fingertips circle the earth over the ether waves of space. He has power. And power is what he wants. He holds dominion over everything upon the face of the earth. Man raises his hand aloft as if to threaten heaven, and shouts that he has gained his dominion, that he controls his destiny. Man is supreme. The hypothetical visitor from another planet might be tempted to ask if man had not confused himself with God. But before the question can be put, there is a sudden blinding flash and devastating explosion. A deafening roar shakes the earth. Man's uplifted hand has been rent to fragments. He is knocked to earth, lies there stunned, his body bleeding and shattered. The very power he has treasured has destroyed the creature which so self-reliantly gathered it. Great buildings are blown to pieces. Bridges are dynamited. Man's ships are torpedoed by the thousands and sunk to the bottom of the ocean. His great airplanes come spinning down from the clouds with tongues of flame engulfing them. And, alas! not only his inventions but his children, his sons and daughters, his fathers and mothers, those whom he was to endow with all this power and might, have been blown to bits by the very power which was to make them rich and forever happy. Man is reduced to a pitiable spectacle. The birds from their perches cheep their derision upon him. The beasts whom he has terrified steal from their forest hide-outs to sneer their glee and contempt. And the fish of the sea rise astonished to the surface to inquire what it is all about.

Man staggers in agony to his feet, to dress his wounds, to seek relief from his suffering. He kneels before the altar, he bows his head to his breast. He raises his question to his God in awe and bewilderment. Was it not God's promise that man should subdue the earth and have dominion over every creature and herd all creation to his own use? Did he not understand aright? Where has man gone wrong? Then Jesus Christ appears to him. Man beholds the compassionate yet piercing eyes of his Lord. Jesus says again, "Thou shalt love the Lord thy God with all thy heart, and with all thy soul, and with all thy mind. This is the first and great commandment. And the second is like unto it. Thou shalt love thy neighbor as thyself."

The Bible has survived the general destruction. The laws of God have not altered since the day the planets were swung into space. But no law is absolute. The law of man's dominion as given by that old Hebrew seer is as true now as it was then. Man was created to have dominion over the fish of the sea, over the fowl of the air and over every living thing that creepeth upon the face of the earth. Jesus came, however, to interpret, to fulfill, to render more clear the way of life. Jesus pointed out another law, the law of co-operation, of brotherhood and love. This law is just as much a law of God, a law of the universe and requires just as much to be heeded as the law of dominion. The two laws complement each other. Man will be eternally confounded in his dominion over the world until he learns and adopts the complementary law, the law of co-operation.

Man has accepted only part of the truth of God. He has vainly imagined that he possessed strength in himself. He has used his powers to rule, to dominate, to command, to control, not only nature but his fellow men. He has built up great states. He has developed super-states or nations. He has put presidents, prime ministers, kings, emperors, even dictators at the head of these nations. He has established his congresses, his parliaments, his reichstags. But too often the motive behind it and the result of it has been scheming, a contest for privilege, for gold, for superior rights. These nations have become but a magnified edition of the individual man with all his selfishness, his greed, his haughtiness. These nations have turned upon each other and they have reached down and taken the individual man to become their slave to do their bidding, to fight their wars, to destroy and make desolate the high places of the earth, the homes, the factories, the fields and the forests, the seas and the oceans, even the temple of God.

Man has used his dominion to gain his own ends. He has even been so abjectly callous that he has condemned his fellow men, his own flesh and blood, to starvation, poverty, disease and death. Natives who lived in the land have been herded into reserves, their forests, their homes, their resources have been stolen from them. They have become indentured labor in their own mines or in their own plantations. What difference does it make if a thousand die ask the masters? They are nothing but "natives." Men have manipulated government and commerce that they might here and there build up vast fortunes and live in ease, but whole nations with millions of inhabitants die without hope of succor in the stench and hovels of subject lands. Men have built economic empires throughout the world. Into great centers of control flows the wealth from the profit taken from others at the point of a gun. The cruelty, the sadism, by which some men have inflicted their rule upon other men are beyond words to express. One shuts his eyes and cannot look longer upon the horror of it. All human imperialism, and monopoly, are parts of the total greed and avarice of man himself. But the power he planned to amass thereby is destroying the very structure designed to contain it.

How mighty is man as he stands there gloating over his achievements and lording it over his fellows. How insignificant is man, how puny, how shrunken he appears as the men he has lorded it over band together and stand before him. Humanity is the real basis for man's dominion.

His dominion has validity only when it serves this humanity. Jesus formulated the law long ago, "He that would be master over you must be as one that serveth."

There is no escape from the condemnation man is under. All of us have sinned. We are guilty together. We have sought ease and comfort for ourselves. We have worshiped a high standard of living but only for ourselves and we have forgotten the poverty of the poor. We have cried "America for Americans" and locked out the Japanese, the Chinese, the Indian, from our shores. We have set up standards for ourselves and, to enforce them, have declared that we can take whatever we want, oil, forests, ores, gold, goods, at our own price and our own terms. We have said to the other nations, "You must buy our surpluses at the price we demand at the time we want to sell them to you." And finally we have been drawn into a world war which had its origins in a challenge to that very economic manipulation and dominance, we are determined to re-establish. Can man never learn? Is he to discover the secrets of all nature and remain in total ignorance of himself? Is he to acquire a multitude of little goods, then to forfeit them all because of his neglect of the greatest good, without which all else is but vanity and an illusion? For his self-punishment and self-destruction will have no end until man is willing to love his neighbor as himself. Until this commandment be learned by heart, all efforts of head and hand are doomed to be ultimately futile.

Imperialisms, monopolies, barriers to trade and all that is part and parcel of them, must be done away with. States and governments must come together in a world federation of nations wherein they will renounce their sovereign power for the good of all. Rights of minorities and majorities must be recognized alike. Free flow of trade and commerce must be instituted. All natural resources must be made equally available. Co-operation and brotherhood must be developed as the basis of all relationships, great and small, narrow and wide. Co-operation is simply religion being worked out in life. Freedom within law, Jesus' idea of true meekness, the love principle in action, the greatest power in the world, are all implied in that single word. The choice before us is co-operation or chaos. Only through love can man gain his dominion over the world. The old Hebrew seer commanded, "Replenish the earth and subdue it and have dominion" and Jesus added, "Thou shalt love the Lord thy God . . . and thy neighbor as thyself." And were a third prophet to appear in our midst today, in wisdom and vision equal to Moses, in love and devotion akin to the Son of God himself, what could he add to that which has so far been delivered? What further could he say but to tell us, "Thou hast already the words of life. This do and thou shalt be saved."

To revert in conclusion to the query with which we started, let us ask again, what is peace? Peace we want, but we want it on our own terms. And this is impossible. Peace is precisely that state of affairs which we cannot have on our own terms. Peace we can have only on God's terms. Peace is that condition man must have if he is to survive. But peace is that condition which man cannot create through his own efforts. We shall never have peace until we cease to play at being gods, and accept God as the Lawgiver of the universe. It is said that the modern man has no god; in a sense this is true. But it is also true that modern man has a god, that his god is himself. Modern man regards the world as exclusively a sphere for his own activity. He vainly imagines he can lay down rules for its operation which suit his convenience and expediencies. It is hard for us to get it through our heads that the structure of things is the same after the Big Three have held a conference as it was before, that the will of God is not subject to alteration by meetings of international statesmen and politicians. But such is the case. The Christian paradox is a stumbling block, but it is immutable. We must pursue our self-interest by co-operation. We must lose our lives to find them.